A Migrant's Musings

A narrative essay

by Alvaro Hernández Blanco

Photographs by the author

To all the wanderers who struggle
to find their place in the world.

INDEX

PROLOGUE

The pigeons in Tijuana are much thinner than in San Diego. They're frail, withered and appear almost sickly. Don't the dimwitted creatures know they can simply take to the skies and fly north but a few miles to indulge in the abundance up there? It's not that there's no food in Tijuana, but rather that what food there is here is not squandered among men like it is *del otro lado.* Over there, pigeons are plump and robust. For them, there's always a hearty meal to scavenge, waiting littered in the street, spilled from a trashcan, peppered across a dump. Some pigeons in San Diego can hardly fly a few seconds before they precipitate to the ground with a desperate flutter because they're so portly. But why choose to fly when you don't have to? You'd only fly when you have somewhere better to be. In Tijuana, what little food litter there is belongs to the insurmountable number of stray dogs that populate the city's landscape. The slight pigeons wouldn't dare challenge them for the remains of a dusty corn tortilla. And so the question persists: why don't the Tijuanense pigeons, unbound to a ground dominated by mangy dogs, just take off and migrate to the land of plenty? They probably ignore its existence altogether. Or maybe they know of it all too well, and conclude that it's simply not worth the trip, all things considered. After all, there's no place like home. Pigeons are as mundane as birds can get. They may not have much going for them, but in a city like Tijuana, the power of flight is a prospect to be envied among much of the human population. The birds' mere presence could drive some folks to the utmost frustration: *"Stupid bird, why are you still here when you could be with your fat cousins?"*

PART ONE

A migrant's musings

1. In tatters.

I loathed the whole process. The paperwork, the lines, the documents - *"we can't use this photo, your eyes are too dark"* –the endless bureaucracy. But I reminded myself: it's a necessary evil. And so I checked in at the front. Time of arrival. Name. Last names. Nationality. *Spaniard.* I browsed the nationality column and found I stuck out like sore thumb among dozens of Haitians, a Colombian, and a couple Chinese fellows. What's a Spaniard doing in Tijuana? It was the first question I was asked upon a local picking up on my Castilian accent. The true response would be long and winded. So I often resolved in replying: *I got lost.* That usually got a laugh. But like all good jokes, there was some truth to it. The Tijuanenses were mostly keen to meet me. Not that I'm that interesting. But I presented a quirky anomaly, sort of like seeing an Eskimo in this dusty border city. *Why would a Spaniard live here? Do you know something we don't?* The Tijuanenses loved their city but were quick to adopt a self-deprecating attitude when comparing their country to the U.S. (*"El otro lado"*, in border lingo) or Europe. They would follow up with: *And how do you like Tijuana?* I couldn't lie and tell them what a beautiful city it was. So I would reply with the diplomatic assertion: *The people are nice. The food is great.* Two statements that I hold to be true.

The line at the immigration office was packed, as it had been for the past few months. A hefty wave of Haitian migrants had arrived in Tijuana in the past year, and they were all looking to formalize their interim stay in Mexico. They were arriving at the border city after a long exodus from Brazil, where many had worked as construction workers while the South American nation revamped its infrastructure in preparation for the 2014 World Cup and the 2016 Olympics. Once those events concluded, Brazil took an economic downturn, and the Haitian nomads knew it was time to move on. Their end game was political asylum in the U.S. They were a strange addition to the demographics of the city, made up of local Tijuanenses, national migrants from the south hoping for better wages, gringo expats looking to stretch their retirement funds, *fresa* hipsters with dual citizenship that permeated the border with their fast passes like they were walking down the street to get milk, and broken deportees who camped along the sad trickle of murky water that is the Tijuana river. Tijuana presented vastly disparate realities to different groups of people. For the crowd of Haitians around me, it seemed to be a pretty nice place. They were fast assimilating into the fabric of the city. They got jobs pumping gas, bagging fruit at the Mercado Hidalgo, and some were even driving Ubers already. They picked up Spanish fast and had an affable demeanor about them. I guess if you grow up in the slums or Port au Prince, Tijuana is considerable upgrade. For all their gratitude toward Mexico, there was one thing: Haitians don't like spicy food. Having rejected Mexican cuisine, some of them had already started to open Haitian chicken joints that were a runaway success among their compatriots. *"De este lado también hay sueños"*, prayed a solemn graffiti on the Mexican side of the border fence. *"On this side, there are dreams too"*. Maybe so.

As I sat in line in the dull waiting room of the migration office, I nervously flicked through my documents, checking that I had every form I needed. *All in order*, I reassured myself, hoping for a swift procedure with the immigration officials. A young man sat beside me. He looked tired, his clothes showed disarray. While I held a plastic folder full of neatly arranged documents, he treasured a single paper that had been folded over and over. I assumed he had carried that form in his pocket for a long time, and I was not wrong. He opened the piece of paper to reveal a Mexican immigration permit in tatters. Some folds had begun to tear, and, in some spots, the printed ink had been smudged by water. *Name: Luis. Nationality: Honduras.* Luis caught me snooping his document and looked at me timidly.

"I hope they accept it. I don't have anything else", he said. His smile was young and nervous, like a schoolboy who's unsure of passing a test. I examined his form again. All the important information seemed to be legible.

"I'm sure you'll be fine", I replied. I was instantly curious about the young man's journey to Tijuana, mainly because my wife is also Honduran, and in the past eight years with her I had become very fond of her country, its towns, its culture, and its people. I couldn't help but pry. "Where in Honduras are you from?"

"Puerto Cortés." I could see he thought that meant nothing to me, but I proved him wrong.

"Ah, I've never been to Puerto Cortés, but I drove past it on my way to Tela", I explained. Tela is a beach town a few miles west of Puerto Cortés on the northern coast of Honduras. His face lit up slightly at the mention of his neighboring town. I knew that feeling. You're lost in the wilderness of the world and some stranger reminds you of your remote hometown. It's as if you're guaranteed that in your journey into the unknown, your home hasn't drifted in the distance into insignificant oblivion. Puerto Cortés is still there, and this funny-sounding stranger bore witness to it.

Luis and I started talking, and quickly I realized that our experiences of Honduras were vastly different. My acquaintance of Tela was from a trip to a beautiful resort with white sand beaches, whereas Luis' departure from Puerto Cortés was catalyzed by the rampant gang violence that had affected him directly. Two accounts, one Honduras: the best of nature spoiled by the worst of men.

He explained that he had travelled through Mexico as part of the migrant caravan that sought to attain political asylum in the U.S. I had heard of said caravan. It struck me that Luis wasn't camping at the border crossing with the rest of the migrants, amidst the attention of international news outlets. Instead, he was at the Tijuana migration office, hoping to process a work permit with which to start functioning in Mexico.

"But aren't you going to the U.S.?" I asked him. He explained that that was his original idea, but he had heard of cases like his own being denied political asylum. This story was familiar to me; Honduran migrants fleeing from some of the most dangerous towns in the Western hemisphere but being denied political asylum because their hometowns were not deemed official 'warzones'. The murder rates may be in the warzone league, but if the innocent deaths are the result of rivaling gangs fighting for turf, trafficking drugs and extorting small businesses, well then, tough luck, but you're not 'political asylum material'. It's not, after all, a strictly political problem. Seen like that, the thought process is not bereft of logic. However, can the issues of a failed state be labeled as political? Policy is rendered futile as the local governments prove incapable of providing solutions of any sort. What Luis was hoping to leave behind was a humanitarian crisis.

"They killed my father and my brother. And if I go back, they will kill me and my family" he said, almost casually. I couldn't imagine myself speaking those words so matter-of-factly. But that had been his reality for a while, so there was no use in being overly dramatic at this point. He had a stoic resolve to look for solutions. However, he knew his fate in the U.S. was uncertain at best. "They ask for proof that you're in danger. How can I prove that? Do I get the *mareros* to sign me a note saying they want to kill me? How can I prove that my father and brother were killed? There is no official paperwork. The gangs own the police, so I have no official reports. The media is too scared to cover any of it. I have nothing."

I couldn't possibly begin to formulate the slightest bit of solace. But I realized he wasn't looking for support. He was just laying out his story. After all, I had asked him where he was coming from. He told me *what* he was coming from, a response that was more than I bargained for. I didn't know Puerto Cortés. I had just read the name on a map.

As we waited to be tended to, Luis told me of his crossing. He had made the trip with his wife and one-year-old daughter. They mostly walked and used freight trains to cross Mexico from south to north. It was a common occurrence for migrants to get on freight trains, which had received the grim moniker of "La Bestia". This bit of migrant lore could be explained by the deafening growling sound the train made as it traverses Mexico's latitude, or by the fact that La Bestia would often fling the miserable stowaways to the tracks, severing their limbs and even killing them. Luis had been lucky to complete the trip unscathed, although he told me he had suffered extreme exhaustion on account of the sleepless nights during which he held his daughter close to his chest to ensure she could sleep safely through the night while her father kept their balance onboard the whooshing deathtrap. Luis remembered those painfully cramped vigils with relief, for the stories of children falling from the train in the dead of the night were too many and too heartbreaking.

For all his care during the trip, Luis had not been able to protect his child from sickness. All those days on the trail under the sun, nights in the street sleeping on the damp ground, and endless hours of that pernicious breeze on La Bestia had taken a toll on the toddler, who now had a fever and was with her mother at the migrant campsite. I asked Luis if he had all he needed to tend to his daughter's sickness.

"I used all the change I had to buy medicine yesterday, but we already finished it. There were more sick children in the caravan", he responded. I gave him the few pesos on me and he thanked me sincerely. "I just want to get a job", he stated sternly, his youthful face becoming more manlike with the weight of his words. Luis was not a poor beggar scrounging for coins, but a man looking to take the reins of his own life and steer it toward prosperity for his loved ones. All he needed was a chance.

And there he was, at the Tijuana migration office, beating La Migra to the punch. He was almost convinced the U.S. would not grant him asylum, and deportation would ensue. In that predicament, Tijuana beat going back to the perils of Honduras. Mexico had been welcoming enough to grant the migrant caravan travelling permits to pass through the country. Now Luis hoped to get his permit upgraded to a proper work visa. The process would probably prove to be more convoluted than Luis could imagine, but the young man had put up with hardships that make any bureaucratic obstacle trivial in comparison.

After our respective appointments, I gave Luis my number, a gesture he could not reciprocate. All his possessions were in a school backpack at the migrant campsite, and there was no cellphone among them. Absurd as it may have been, I insisted that he could call me if he thought I could help him. *Godspeed, Luis.* We shook hands and parted ways.

2. Left alone.

That afternoon I received a call from Martha, a client for whom I had produced numerous food-related videos. Incidentally, she was calling about the migrant caravan in Tijuana. She had sent a team of reporters to get some human-interest stories from the migrants, but the freelance reporters ended up selling their piece to a higher bidder. Martha then asked me if I'd be interested to take on those videos for her. I agreed, looking forward to stepping out of my comfort zone. Most of the videos I produced for her were colorful video recipes for social media platforms. They had become my bread and butter but at this point were too routinary to pose interesting challenges. I missed the days of pointing my camera at people and being told a fascinating story.

I drove to the San Ysidro crossing and found a makeshift camp full of migrant families, volunteers and numerous reporters like myself. The camp was situated right at the entrance of the border crosswalk. *'Aquí empieza la patria'*, read a sign for people who had just entered Mexico from the U.S. It was the motto of the city of Tijuana, and I never knew if it was meant as a proud slogan or just the plain statement of a geographical fact. True to Tijuana's ambivalence, it worked both ways.

Over the last few days, the camp had become a lively microcosm buzzing with activity. There was an area where children played, a stand where volunteers served donated food, a small marquee where first aid was administered, and dozens of tents in which entire families passed time talking, playing or napping. The place was extremely busy but appeared clean and organized. It seemed like most migrants knew one another at this point, and the children of different families mingled and played as if they'd been friends for years, like neighbors without a neighborhood to call their own. I was a little apprehensive about entering the camp. It was their current home, but there was no door to knock on. I went in and started asking around. I hit it off with a man named David Salgado, from Tegucigalpa, Honduras. He seemed to know everyone from the caravan pretty well, and I asked if he would be my field producer for the day, introducing me to some of his fellow migrants that would be willing to share their testimony. He agreed, happy to do something different for a change; for most of the migrants, the days spent camping in the streets of Tijuana had become a tedious waiting game. However, David confessed he believed most would prefer the days of wait over the uncertain future that lay ahead once the U.S. finally beckoned them to walk across the border.

"We have come here to beg to the toughest and coldest man on Earth", he assured me.

"Trump?" I asked. He simply nodded gravely, as if he didn't want to say the name himself. It was easy to see why. The mere mention of it brought discouragement to the hopeful spirit of the campsite. American immigration lawyers who had crossed into Tijuana to work pro-bono walked among the tents and gave tips to each of the travelers. The gringos gave them do's and don'ts, told them what to expect, and assured them that even though the odyssey through Mexico was over, the bureaucratic battle ahead would not be any easier. It was said that, while their cases were examined, men would be detained at immigration camps, while women would be allowed to go on something like a parole, with a GPS device tied to their ankles so they wouldn't leave a predetermined area. As for the group of transsexual women who were fleeing from hate crimes, who knew what deal they'd get. Uncertainty loomed over the campsite, and conversations divided the migrants between those brooding skepticism and those positive they would soon be living the American Dream.

David introduced me to several of his migrant friends. Many of them were happy to chat with me but turned down a filmed interview. These simple men had led discreet lives in their home countries and now found themselves amidst a media storm where politics played a big part. They didn't want to be made into the poster boys of so-and-so's party. They didn't want media outlets simply capitalizing on their plight and turning their stories into sensationalism –the morbid details of a lot of their stories could become sensationalism of the lowest order. I tried hard to convey an earnest interest on my part to simply give them and outlet to send a message that would do their story justice. I finally met a woman from El Salvador named Isabel. She initially rejected my interview because she was tidying up her tent and tending to her children. I left her to her chores and looked elsewhere, but after about thirty minutes she caught up to me and tapped me on the shoulder.

"I'm ready now", she said with a candid smile. She had visibly groomed herself to appear particularly presentable before the camera. If someone had told me this lady had just hiked across one of the biggest countries on Earth, I would not have believed them. The same could be said for the rest of the camp. In spite of camping out in the street with no direct access to running water, everyone there seemed to put great efforts into keeping clean and dignified. Wet wipes and hand-sanitizer were in high demand at the donations stand, and migrants would wander into the streets of Tijuana to find laundromats to wash the few clothes that were at this point their only possessions.

Isabel and I found a quiet corner where we conducted the interview. She spoke with melancholy of her abandoned country, projecting a vivid image of a place that she once loved but which had recently transformed into her personal living hell. She had brought her two children along with her, and they had spurred her on during the toughest parts of the migration. While we spoke, Isabel's children played on mats on the floor a few feet away from us, one with a puzzle and the other with cards. Isabel looked at them with glassy eyes.

"They're good boys. Like all boys, they just want to play, and go to school, and draw, and play ball, and learn. We just want a place where they can do that and be left alone". She spoke of how the *maras* would often recruit boys around their age and quickly turn them into criminals. Isabel was relieved to have left all that behind her, but also asserted: "I wish they hadn't seen some of the things they saw".

She shook her head gently, her eyes focusing on nothing at this point. I asked her what she did back home.

"I had a bakery, but had to close it down. The gangs kept extorting me for money, so I ended up shutting it down. I was living in fear and not making money anymore. *¿Pues pa qué?*"

Remembering had made Isabel gloomy and I tried to inject some levity into the conversation.

"Can you make pupusas? 'Cause those are popular in Southern California."

"That I can do! *Y muy ricas*", she said as she patted an invisible pupusa between her weathered hands.

As we talked, Isabel slowly lifted the veil of her backstory, delving into some painful admissions of her own life. As it turned out, one of the kids that came with her wasn't really her son, but that of her daughter. I would've never guessed it, as Isabel was in that ambiguous age where old mothers intersect with young grandmothers. I imagined my *abuelas* enduring an exodus through México with seven-year-old me. *Not a chance.* Isabel lowered her voice and leaned in closer, her eyes on her grandchild playing with the puzzle.

"Javier was the result of my daughter being raped", she whispered. "His father is a *salvatrucha* leader. It's horrible". Isabel explained that her daughter desperately sought an abortion, an idea that always struck Isabel as inhumane. *"¿Pues qué culpa tenía el niño?" How is it the baby's fault?* The rapist father also threatened the mother-to-be into getting an abortion and doing so as soon as possible. Isabel's stance was aided by the illegality of abortion in El Salvador, and she had been convincing enough to lure her daughter away from back-alley procedures. Isabel also compelled her daughter not to give up the baby for adoption, as that fate was also uncertain. Leaving an underfunded and chaotic Salvadoran orphanage was not guaranteed, let alone winding up in a good foster family. Isabel took it upon herself to raise the baby as her own, much to her daughter's objection. She couldn't bear to have the baby around. Not only would the mere act of having the baby go against the father's threats. She also couldn't stand to look into her child's eyes and see his rapist father. Nonetheless, Isabel was adamant about keeping the newborn. "He is blood of our blood", she would insist, and with undeterred conviction, took the baby under her wing. However, her play didn't quite pan out as she had hoped.

"I haven't seen my daughter in seven years. She doesn't want anything to do with the poor child".

Isabel lost a daughter to save a baby. The scars of that painful episode were palpable in her longing eyes. But she remained optimistic.

"If God grants me the possibility of living in the States, I would like to reach out to my daughter and ask her to join me. She is still living in a very dangerous area. I hope she will take my hand and join us where we can all live in peace, *si Dios nos da licencia..."*

3. License.

"Si Dios nos da licencia". That expression always packed a punch with me. *If God grants us license.* I had often heard it from people who had been put to the test in ways I couldn't fathom. I didn't know if it was a prayer or a request for permission to pursue something. I had first heard the expression (which doesn't exist in my native Castilian Spanish) in Los Angeles, a city that I called my home for three years. I arrived there as a twenty-two-year-old student looking to get a foot in the door of the entertainment industry. I started off getting gigs as a video editor. As a modest entry-level professional, my first apartment in L.A. was in a working-class *barrio*, where I was plunged into the vibrant Mexican culture. At first, I was wary about living in the so-called 'dangerous' parts of town, as they said, but I soon found I felt closer to home in those areas than in the parts of L.A. where they worshipped avocados and put their dogs in special pet spas. There was a comforting familiarity about the Hispanic community surrounding me. Perhaps they didn't have much, but they had their priorities straight in a town were few people had both feet firmly on the ground.

On a typical weekend, Smiley Drive would be filled with the alluring smell of *carne asada* and the sounds of heartfelt *rancheras* and *piñatas* being bashed in. I would often take strolls in the area, just to enjoy the ambience coming from those homes. The kids playing with their bikes in the street, hoping to catch a *raspado* vendor; the bouncy castle that inevitably led to some kid getting projected violently to the ground before he ran wailing to his mom; and the occasional fireworks that would result in an LAPD helicopter circling the area, spotlight shining down upon us. The intense shaft of brightness would often find me sitting on my lawn chair, sipping from a lime *Jarritos*, while I looked up at the night sky with a grin. I loved Smiley Drive.

It was in this time that I first heard the phrase *"si Dios nos da licencia"*. I distinctly remember the episode, which took place in the small supermarket on Adams Blvd., parallel to Smiley Drive. It was a typically torrid summer day in Los Angeles and I thought I would head to the store to indulge in a refreshing treat. I approached the entrance, a tough dilemma occupying my mind (should I go for the horchata or the watermelon paleta?), when I saw Margarita in the parking lot sobbing uncontrollably. Margarita was one of the cashiers that worked in the supermarket. She was a stout Salvadoran woman in her forties, and over the months I had become fond of her chipper disposition at the checkout aisle. But today she was weeping, her overstated makeup running astray.

"*¿Qué pasó, Margarita?* What's the matter?" I inquired.

"My husband was supposed to cross today. He was supposed to give me a call in the morning. It's been hours and I haven't heard from him yet".

By crossing, of course, she meant unlawfully sneaking into the U.S. This was not a *no-news-good-news* scenario. Endless events could turn the border crossing into a nightmare, the lightest of which would be simply getting caught by border patrol. On the more grim end of the spectrum was dying a slow and blistering death under the blazing Sonoran sun, getting caught up in cartel violence, being beaten, robbed and left to die by the *polleros*, or suffocating inside the hidden nooks and crannies of a tanker truck. With all this in mind, I thought it would be tone-deaf to ask about the details of Margarita's husband's crossing.

"Give it a few more hours. It could just be bad reception. He'll be here with you soon", I said, trying hard to believe my words.

"I hope so, *si Dios nos da licencia*".

On my way home, (watermelon *paleta* in hand), I mulled those words over. *If God grants us license.* It was almost as if God was the ultimate puppet-master behind of all those hostile factors that governed the desert. Only He could clear the way with a fell swoop of providence. But what was even more striking was that Margarita was essentially imploring God to facilitate an illegal act. When I was young, I was told I shouldn't pray for my soccer team to win. In what I later discovered to be a considerable theological fallacy, I was told: *"God doesn't have time for soccer"*. I got it; don't pray for such unimportant things. But praying so you can break the law and get away with it? Boy, that was really pushing it. But then again, maybe God disregarded borderlines that were the result of ancient human conflict. Heck, guiding people through the desert has always been God's thing –among other godly affairs. The human conventions that disavowed this particular crossing probably meant nothing to Him. I thought I was reaching a conclusion: crossing an imaginary line in the desert is not a sin. But then... what of rendering unto Caesar what is Caesar's? Wasn't that a call to respect the manmade laws that regulated society? The splintery wooden stick at the end of my *paleta* pulled me out of my ruminations.

Some months after that, my time in LA was rapidly coming to an end. I had stretched my student visa as long as I could, but was ultimately unable to find a sponsor who would vouch for me with a full-fledged work visa. I found myself in a frustrating predicament, as there was no shortage of people who would want to hire me as a producer and editor. But once I raised the not-so-small issue of my need of a work visa, the talks quickly fizzled out.

"That's too bad" the potential employer would say, "but be sure to check in with us once you *do* get your visa. We'd love to work with you in the future." I didn't hold it against them. A visa implied a tedious immigration case and dealing with lawyers and the government was expensive and slow. In many cases, that investment of time and resources went to waste, as the government decided that, ultimately, the U.S. had no *real* need for you. And it would probably be true. In Hollywood, no-one is irreplaceable.

After much back and forth, my wife and I decided to move from Los Angeles to Tijuana, much to our family and friends' dismay. We were fully aware of the connotations Tijuana had: ran down, chaotic, poor, and, last but not least, dangerous. And heck, for all we knew, all that was true. But we had visited the city twice, and we knew Tijuana had something else going for it. It was a strategic hub from which to work for the US market while living a very affordable life. Getting papers in México would not pose such a problem for us, as the country is known for what is pejoratively known as *malinchismo*. Named after the infamous Nahuatl woman La Malinche, who is said to have betrayed the indigenous peoples of Tenochtitlan by cozying up to the conquistadors to work as their translator, *malinchismo* refers to Mexico's habit of favoring foreigners over their own people. I should specify that *malinchismo* doesn't benefit *any* foreigner, but mostly those from countries that, in general terms, are faring better than Mexico. Of course, *malinchismo* is not an official policy, but it is an idea that tacitly permeates Mexico's relations with the world. Be that as it may, my wife (who holds a French passport) and I, the forsaken Spaniard, eventually attained our papers to settle in Tijuana. The process was tedious and longwinded, but the obstacles were purely bureaucratic. In the U.S., visa cases are more swiftly resolved, although more often than not, said resolution is a cold rejection.

4. One's worth.

Around the time when my wife and I decided to move to Tijuana, I broke the news to an American friend of mine, who lamented:

"Man, it sucks that good people like you can't stay here to live and work while so many illegals break into the country".

I appreciated the sympathy, but I was at odds with his words. It was a strange assertion, one the essentially projected the immigration phenomenon as a zero-sum game: if an undocumented immigrant sneaks into the U.S., it will ultimately be at the expense of a person who wishes to move there lawfully. To this day, I don't know the level of truth there is to the statement. Yes, the bigger the influx of illegal immigrants, the more rigid immigration laws become. But I couldn't possibly look at, say, Carlos the janitor, and believe in my heart of hearts he was taking my place in the U.S.

"It's not like that", I assured my friend. "I wouldn't trade places with those folks. To be honest, I don't think I have what it takes".

"What do you mean?" my friend asked.

I tried to organize the thoughts in my head. To a degree, the idea of illegal migration was an alluring one, if only because legal migration was such a headache. It's a labyrinth of endless paperwork, ever-increasing expenses, and an excruciating level of uncertainty. When all is said and done on your part, your case –a bunch of papers that aims to convey why you are a valuable addition to the country- is shipped of to USCIS to undergo the most opaque and mysterious of evaluations in the turf of The Man himself. There, the legitimacy of a person's case (and ultimately the worth of that person altogether in the eyes of the U.S.) is judged in a number of different ways through a system that aims to constitute a meritocracy, but is not without its shortcomings.

For instance, if you possess tremendous wealth, the obtaining of a U.S. visa should not pose a problem. You may well be a dim-witted knucklehead with little to no business acumen, and all your wealth could be inherited. It doesn't matter. The U.S. is interested in those succulent accounts. You're in.

The system also rewards notoriety of any kind. Showmanship goes a long way in the eyes of USCIS. The type of show you put on and its rightful place in society are completely secondary concerns –if they are concerns at all. You could be a narcissistic instagrammer prone to pouting, hold the record for most pancakes flipped in a minute, be a prolific adult film actor with a filmography in the hundreds, a scandalous modern artist who likes to put dead animals in formol... I've even met people who created their own religion in order to obtain a religious visa. Of course, these are eccentric fringe cases, but my point stands true; if you are good at that thing you do, and you make good money doing it, USCIS will put a sticker on your passport. One can only hope more stickers are awarded to brain surgeons than to the aforementioned profiles.

The U.S. visa phenomenon is all at once fair, absurd, arbitrary, and farcical. It is also routinely abused by all parties involved. Many visa applicants have cheated the system through so-called anchor babies and sham greencard marriages. On the other end, the U.S. government had been known to hand out very dubious visas in pursuit of ulterior goals, most infamously to Nazi officials whose ghastly resumés were deemed valuable in the light of that era's newest threat: Soviet communism. Notorious is the case of Wernher von Braun, the Nazi engineer who designed the rocket bombs that reduced London to a pile of rubble and death. His expertise in the field of jet propulsion was, as it turned out, a highly regarded asset for the US government at the dawn of the Space Race, so the CIA briskly handed von Braun a ticket to the U.S. before he could face any serious repercussions for his involvement in the Nazi Wehrmacht. Likewise, Nazi spies who during the war had garnered information on the soviets suddenly found themselves recruited by American government agencies to carry on their anti-communist pursuits, -this time under the red, white and blue.

Finally, sponsors also abuse the visa phenomenon customarily by acquiring visas for employees hailing from third world countries, employees who in turn can only work for said sponsor. This means the worker has no leverage against his employer, as his residence in the U.S. is entirely dependent on that company's consent to have them. Simply put, there's no room to ask for a raise, demand better conditions, or –least of all- yell a cathartic *'I quit'*. In those scenarios, your employer would quite literally send you packing.

When it comes to U.S. visas and all the phenomena that relate to them, one can only throw up his hands and profess that tired adage: *it is what it is.* With all that laid out, the question is: do you want to play along? And how do you fancy your chances of having your visa approved? If you're a young professional like myself with little more than a college degree and a few years of experience, the game is liable to turn sour very quick, as my wife and I experienced when our two expensive attempts at visas were rejected. If you're a coffee-picker from Central America, a construction worker from Oaxaca, or a primary school teacher from Zacatecas, the game is almost entirely out of your league. One often hears undocumented immigrants are skipping in front of all the people in line to migrate legally. Undocumented migrants therefore should *'get to the back of the line'*. The fallacy here is that, for most of those folks, there simply is no line, as their options to migrate legally are almost entirely non-existent.

There is, however, a seasonal worker's visa for migrants to work in the agriculture industry, carrying out jobs Americans are unwilling to fill. In that aspect, it's not too far from the types of jobs undocumented migrants usually take on, but the visa lasts only a few months before the workers are sent back home. This type of visa has been contentious, as they only last a few months and once they expire, many workers choose to simply escape into the vastness of the U.S. territory and live out their days surreptitiously attempting the American dream. I had considered this route myself, if only for a fleeting second. At face value, it was a romantic idea. However, life would present a much more ominous reality for those dreamers that chose to ignore their geopolitical curfew.

"Heck, I could become an *illegal* too, if I wanted." I told my friend. "It is as easy as overstaying my welcome. It's the life that follows that's the tough part. I couldn't do it."

He listened as I unraveled what I had witnessed after three years of living among such migrants in LA. Indeed, the closer I got to the undocumented immigrant community in California, the more I learned that the idea of the American Dream was hole-punched full of caveats for them. Long were the days of entering the U.S. under the kind-hearted gaze of the Statue of Liberty and going from a downtrodden nomad to a millionaire business tycoon in a matter of a few decades. This new American dream could have little to no return on investment for its protagonists, but that was fine by them, as they stoically took on the roles of lonesome pioneers in what they hoped would become an inspiring family saga for the ages.

The American dream as it pertained to those humble Hispanic migrants demanded heart-wrenching sacrifice and a type of abnegation that would simply not make sense in the eyes of more self-centered individuals. In a Western culture that celebrates excessive materialism, instant gratification of the self, and attaining personal success before considering others, the migrant's edifying philosophy would prove a defiant anomaly from which much could be learned, but which society instead chose to abuse. This selflessness is what drove many migrants to accept the country's lowest wages and occupy rental rooms by the dozen. They lived in extreme frugality, maximizing any left-over dollars to wire them abroad to their homes, or to afford the odd treat for the wife and children accompanying them in their odyssey. I told my friend that not only did I not resent those so-called illegals, but that I tipped my hat to them in admiration. If only visas were handed out on the merits of hard work, generosity and sacrifice. Aren't those traits upon which to build a strong nation?

Living the American Dream was no bed of roses when it had to be done under the radar. Stories of families being apprehended by immigration enforcement authorities circulated the grapevine on a daily basis and haunted the migrants in their sleep. It wasn't uncommon for undocumented migrants to neglect getting medical attention or seeking help from the police and other local authorities, as they feared that any surfacing in official records could spark a process that would end with their deportation. Needless to say, going back to their home countries for things such as medical treatment was out of the question, as they would have to risk life and limb once more to sneak back into American soil. That's not to say one can only be a *mojado* once. I once met a man in Brooklyn named Jesús. He was a Mexican immigrant who had been deported twice, and simply returned the same way he had come in the first time. He told the story casually, underlining the absurd comedy of the events and underplaying the merit in his feat. He was well aware of the types of awed reactions his narration would elicit. Third time was the charm for him, and today he runs a popular *taquería* in the gentrified neighborhood of Bushwick. His story, however, is not the norm, as *mojados* typically do everything in their power to avoid having to repeat that infernal journey into forbidden land.

"*La Jaula de oro*", -the golden cage- was a term commonly used by undocumented migrants to refer to the U.S.. When compared to their home countries, everything in the U.S. was shiny and modern. But they couldn't help but feel caged in by the lives they had chosen to live in the U.S., away from their families and cultures, and amidst a growing sense that their kind wasn't welcome. The land that had once prided itself in giving refuge to *"the tired, the poor, and huddled masses yearning to breathe free",* now seemed to say *"Sorry, we're full and have enough problems of our own. Don't come knocking."* But the poor and tired migrants kept on arriving, assured that whatever mistreatment they were liable to encounter in the U.S. would be merely anecdotal in comparison to the humanitarian crisis they were leaving behind in their home countries. This is not to say their vital plights were over –far from it! Like a heavy-laden donkey treading uphill behind a carrot dangling from a stick, these migrants found an equally elusive incentive to press on: *hope*. Hope that their future generations would have it much better. It was a trans-generational vow, a pact with destiny to forfeit one's own life in the hopes that future descendants may benefit from the sweat and tears of their ancestors. The devotion many migrants displayed to St. Jude Thaddeus had its reasons: he was, after all, the patron saint of hope and lost causes.

Nothing was certain about these migrants' plan, and all they could do was keep their heads down and bust their backs picking strawberries or scrubbing toilets for the rest of their days. Maybe the pioneering migrants would not get to experience the wonders of the U.S. in all of its glorious abundance. But still they ploughed ahead, confident that the callus in their hands would be the seed to a brighter future to be harvested by generations down the line.

In many cases, the unforgiving melting pot that is the U.S. and the implacable passage of time would murk the descendants' ability to cast their sights back to honor the family's pioneer and profess: *"We made it. Gracias."* In the same manner, many of the migrants would never live to see the fruits of their sacrifice, and those who did oftentimes would be invaded by a sense of inadequacy they never foresaw when they initiated the family exodus. They looked at their grandchildren who talked, behaved and lived like any other American kid, and it would all feel... well, foreign. To add to this bitter realization, the old-timer migrants often witnessed helplessly how their grandchildren were raised entirely in English. Many migrant families were so focused on their kids' integration in the U.S. that they begin to see the knowledge of the Spanish language as a possible social hindrance. After all, in many areas of the U.S., Spanish is regarded as low class, and thus the new American children are made to cut ties with the language of Cervantes, Márquez and Neruda.

These were the *pochos*, which literally translates as *rotten*, a term used among Hispanics to refer to the generations who are irremediably disconnected from the Hispanic culture of their forefathers. The expression always struck me as tough and demeaning, but upon closer inspection it revealed vivid and truthful metaphor. It seemed to me that the *pochos* were rotten because they had been detached from the tree for so long. The vital sap that rose from the roots was not making it to the figurative fruits that were the new generations. The Mexican grandfather who had worked for decades to lead his Mexican family to prosperity now realized that, somewhere along the way, the Mexican part got lost in the shuffle. What was supposed to become an epic family saga simply diluted into anonymity. All that remained was a Spanish last name, devoid of *tildes* and memory.

5. Mestizaje.

Closely related to the term *pocho* was another Spanish word used extensively when discussing matters of migration: *desarraigo*. The term literally means *rootlessness* and is the cause for the existentialist solitude many migrants experience when they realize their newfound land will never feel like home, and that they've been away from their native countries for so long that when they go back, it no longer feels like home either. *"Ni de aquí ni de allá".* (*"Not from here, nor from there"*). It is the dreadful realization that your family, community, town, city and nation have inexorably moved on without you, and that they do not need you or miss you nearly as much as you need and miss them.

El desarraigo comes in many gradients. In my personal case, as a migrant who could at any given moment decide to return home, it was the constant evaluating of the cost of opportunity. At every turn in my time abroad, I found myself thinking: *am I happier than if I were back home? Are the good things here worth living so far from my loved ones?* My destinations -Los Angeles and then Tijuana- proved to be a strategic places for my professional aspirations, but I found them lacking in just about every other aspect of the overall *calidad de vida* (quality of life). On the other hand, my home country, Spain, still bore the scars of the global recession that afflicted it more deeply than most countries in Europe. Salaries were low, and jobs in creative fields were scarce. And yet, at times, I found Spain to be better fitted than the U.S. or México to carry out a balanced and fulfilled life. *Maybe.* And so the questions persisted, all amounting to the mother of all interrogations: *All things considered, what should be my place in the world?* My particular *desarraigo* projected a series of *what-ifs* that I struggled hard not to entertain, for therein lied madness. I always resolved in putting off my eventual return to Spain after I had acquired more personal growth overseas, wherever that may be. The strange part of the *desarraigo* is that at times it strikes you as a gradual loss of identity, whereas in other cases being a migrant in foreign lands is most certainly conducive to more acute self-definition. Your oneness as an individual is affirmed once you have been removed from the community with which you share so many things. Contrast is good for self-definition, as at every turn you inevitably find yourself reacting to an environment you do not take for granted because you did not grow up in it. This is by no means a negative thing, as you are forced to revise your ideas and convictions instead simply drifting with the worldview you are born into.

As a fruit of this process, I found myself unconsciously and slowly constructing in my mind the fundaments, if simplistic and half-baked, for what I reckoned would be an ideal society. I arrived at conclusions such as: *'American trains should be better'* and *'Spanish car rentals should be cheaper'*. The thoughts often came coupled, like *'I think Americans should take more holidays'* and *'I guess Spaniards should take less holidays'*, each wishful thought projecting an area of betterment from the parallel reality of another nation's idiosyncrasy. My native Spain and the U.S. presented manners of living most developing countries would strive to emulate, although it was said that in the former people work to live, with in the latter people live to work. It is unclear to me if these fundamentally different mindsets are at the chore of the culture or rather are the manifestation of centuries of sociological tensions and policies and an infinite number of variables unique to those territories. Both are probably true to an extent that is impossible to decipher.

Where did Mexico fare in all of these mental projections of mine? Mexico, for all of its shortcomings, occupied a sweet spot in my heart. In spite of all its pitfalls and imperfections, (including but not limited to its notoriously corrupt government, the much-aggrandized bureaucracy, the countless areas of insecurity, and a generalized inefficiency in the service industry), Mexico presented a refreshing *joie de vivre*. It wasn't the type of innocent merriment that stems from the maxim *'ignorance is bliss'*. On the contrary, I believed Mexicans' appreciation for a life well-lived had more to do with the country's constant reminders of evil forces lurking around every corner. Misery, injustice, and violence loomed over the patches of land they didn't govern outright. With such grim realities baked into the social fabric of the country, many a Mexican resolved in simply cohabiting with these dreaded life companions while singing life's praises where they could. In Mexican lore, death is hardly a taboo. Instead, it is celebrated in joyful festivities. There is the famous Día de Muertos, in which families commemorate their deceased adorning altars with their photographs and their favorite dishes. Around this date, it is common to see a colorful folkloric character making the rounds; La Calavera Catrina, (The Dapper Skull), a skeleton lady clad in colorful festive garments.

It is also an esteemed tradition among Mexicans to write so-called *calaveritas literarias,* a form of short poetry that encapsulates ridiculous epitaphs aimed at friends and family, entailing burlesque and spooky depictions of their demise. When I first heard about these long-established poems, I was taken aback by the concept. How could you dedicate to a loved one a text describing their death? It was upon reading a few of them that I was won over by their undeniable charm. *Calaveritas literarias* often included, in a humorous tone, little tales of the protagonist's untimely death as caused by an exaggerated depiction of that person's faults or misconduct. They were, in essence, very personalized and humorous cautionary tales. The rhyming and almost cartoonish representation of the deathly elements made it all come together in a quintessentially Mexican concoction.

For the aforementioned reasons, an outsider might consider some aspects of Mexican culture grim and sordid. Having lived in Mexico for some years now, I can attest that the opposite is true. Mexican lore is not bereft of dark iconography, but its unnerving nature is always spiced with proverbial Mexican sarcasm and ingenuity that give even the grimmest of elements a rather amenable levity. Where other Western cultures approach the topics of death and suffering with the utmost shock and solemnity, Mexico's response is more natural in its earnestness, based on the unfaltering knowledge that death and suffering are simply constants in life, not unlike joy and love. Of course, this worldview has everything to do with the country's deeply Catholic roots and belief in a world to come. In many conversations with Mexican folk, I found that such belief systems were prevalent even among individuals who did not consider themselves religious in the rigorous sense. It wasn't, at this point, the Church's eschatology, but Mexico's independent take on the matter. In this sense, Mexican culture was warmer and more comforting than that of most Western nations. It seemed to me that Mexicans took life exactly as seriously as it ought to be taken, not an ounce more or less.

Another reason for which I had grown to love Mexico there was the endless traces of Spain present in its vivid and eclectic culture, born out of the clash of two vastly different worlds; the old Judeo-Christian Europe and the newly found Mesoamerican civilizations. When regarding Mexico's uniquely colorful traditions, it was easy to romanticize the *mestizaje* that sparked the nation's genesis. The flipside to that, however, was the prevailing classism that permeated the country centuries after the conquistadors' arrival in Veracruz. Mexican society was still very much divided into those from a predominantly indigenous gene pool, and those with fair skin –or *'güeros'*. It wasn't unusual in Mexico to hear phrases such as *'¡No seas indio!' ('Don't be an Indian!')*, meant as a warning against crude and uneducated behavior. Many Mexicans, I found, were at odds with the foundational reality of their nation, at once showing disdain for the indigenous peoples and professing contempt for Spain's indelible footprint in their land. As Nobel laureate Octavio Paz wrote, the Mexican identity is not so much based on the mix of two worlds, but rather the negation of them. This position seemed unsustainable, as I reckoned that any attempt at a sense of identity that sought to do away with this fateful clash of cultures was flimsy. It either demanded longwinded mental gymnastics, or indeed required no thinking at all.

That being said, I understood the general sentiment of those who thought that way, even if it put on display a very low-resolution understanding of an extremely nuanced topic that spanned centuries. The summation of such thinking could be; *"The indigenous people were mostly brutish, while the Spaniards were mostly keen on pillaging and raping; us Mexicans are something else."* Such broad statements were problematic not just because of the gross generalizations put forward, but also because they somehow implied an essential detachment between those two civilizations and the resulting Mexican nation as we now know it, as if the Mexico had been born out of the Big Bang, with nothing to precede it. This could not be further from the truth.

In my first visit to the once capital of New Spain (Mexico City), I came upon a plaque that perfectly summarized Mexico's genesis. It was located in la *Plaza de las Tres Culturas (The Square of the Three Cultures)*, named after the two civilizations that clashed to create a new one. The plaque read:

On the 13th of August, 1521

Though heroically defended by Cuauhtemoc,

Tlatelolco fell in the grasp of Hernan Cortés

It was neither triumph nor defeat,

But the painful birth of the mixed people

That is today's Mexico.

This beautifully and plainly stated summary of such a fateful date was common knowledge among Mexicans, at least at an academic level. But when it came to identity, -that is, when it came to what Mexicans actually felt-, many did not *de facto* share this take on history, instead choosing to adopt a dubious ambivalence. They would indeed proclaim that date to be either a triumph or a defeat. A growing pro-indigenist movement had driven many Mexicans to deride Spain's empire in its entirety, while others continued to tout their European roots to perpetuate the sort of classism that kept Mexican indigenous people in disenfranchisement. These attitudes were mainstream and, much to my surprise, individuals who helmed them were quick to flip-flop to whatever side was convenient to them depending on the discussion being held.

I once visited a barbershop in Los Angeles where I was tended to by a perfectly affable Mexican. Being the type of customer that likes to partake in friendly conversation, I started to make small talk, asking him about the area, his business, where he came from, etc. He engaged in detail with a courtly demeanor. After a few minutes speaking, he picked up on my accent and guessed that I was from Argentina -a common mistake among Mexicans and Central Americans, I had found.

"Spain, actually," I corrected him.

"Oh... Spain," he replied softly.

There was a beat of silence, and then it started.

"Is it nice over there?" he inquired.

"Oh, it's beautiful," I said, inadvertent to what was to come.

"I bet it is! You stole all our gold! You took our jewels and our art!"

I was at once stumped at the sudden change of tone and bemused at his choice of words. His use of the first and the second person made an ancient conflict appear fresh and personal between two individuals who had just met in the 21st century.

Being that at this point he was shaving the stubble on my neck by gently scraping it with a razor, I decided to adopt a role for the remaining duration of the haircut. The new me, as far as the vindictive Mexican barber was concerned, would be a self-deprecating *woke* millennial.

"Yes... I guess we did steal your gold", I capitulated.

"And now my country is poor because of yours", he becried.

Such a statement warranted a lengthy debate, but I chose instead to acquiesce.

"Yes. It is a real shame. I'm very sorry," I replied.

The accusations went on casually as he proceeded to cut my hair.

"You took our gold and left us lousy mirrors..." *Flick-flick.* "You brought us disease..." he sighed heavily as he wet my hair with a sprayer.

One would think it was not me, but Hernán Cortés himself sitting there on that padded gyrating chair, while Moctezuma loomed over him with a comb in one hand and an obsidian razor in the other. I frightfully wondered just how far back the chair could recline, and if doing so would leave me in a more propitious position for my still-beating heart to be harvested with one thumping swoop of the obsidian blade.

For a while, I endured the surreal accusations, caught in between a state of awkwardness and frustration that I couldn't be a spectator in this bizarre comedy instead of its hapless protagonist. At the mercy of my plaintiff barber, the haircut proceeded with normalcy, but with such tension in the air that my mind irremediably evoked Sweeney Todd imagery. In my mind, the barber's stance didn't make a whole lot of sense; he was essentially identifying himself as an Aztec and me as an imperialist conquistador. But in the 21ˢᵗ century, conquistadors no longer existed, let alone Aztecs. Perhaps, I told myself, it was precisely the fact that Aztecs were defeated and made to disappear that drove the barber to vindicate them by identifying as one. Of course, it was merely a romanticized sort of identification, and I realized that us Spaniards, in turn, do this sort of thing as well; the Celt city of Numantia, (whose ruins reside in northern Spain), is today regarded as a symbol for Spanish resilience, pride and spunk. It fought off endless Roman legions, up until the exasperated empire decided to send in Scipio Aemilianus, its greatest general, to take care of the pesky situation. Aware of the Celts' relentless bravado, he decided to besiege the city instead of attacking it. After more than a year, the Celts who hadn't starved to death killed themselves instead of going through the humiliation of surrender. More than two thousand years later, Numantia remains a symbol for Spanish grit and determination among Spaniards, a people whose existence has been much more heavily influenced and shaped by the Roman empire than by the Celts. After all, Spanish is a romance language (read *Roman*) and Catholicism was the religion inherited from the Roman empire. So, what sense does it make to retrospectively root for the Celts and their little mountain city of Numantia? It's handy to chop up history into little episodes and avoid going through the extenuating mental exercise of seeing the big picture, as doing so may drive us to the realization that we descend from the very people we claim are the *bad guys*, and not the courageous underdogs we like to idealize, be they Celts or Aztecs. In fact, it would be a stretch to call the Aztecs the underdogs, because a quick look at Hernán Cortés' campaign will suffice to realize that, if there was an underdog in the battle for Tenochtitlan, it was the conquistadors who played away from home with a much smaller regiment. But you can't claim an overwhelming victory and retain the 'underdog' category –not when you've totally and irrevocably ended a powerful empire. Perhaps history shouldn't be regarded in such Manichean terms; history is not a movie populated by good guys and villains. Like the human spirit itself, it tends to be full of grey area.

Much to my relief, the barber and I managed to move on from the subject of the conquest of the Americas by the crown of Castile in the 16th century. The barber now took an interest in modern day Spain.

"You know, I got word that if you have a Spanish last name, you may file for Spanish citizenship!" he exclaimed.

"That so?"

"So I hear! And I have a Spanish last name: *Valencia*", he said with aplomb.

I knew exactly what he was referring to. A few months before, the government of Spain had announced that it would grant Spanish citizenship to those who could prove they descended from the Sepharad Jewish community, which, beginning in 1492, had been forced to choose between conversion to Christianity and exile. This catalyzed a diaspora whereby many Spanish-speaking Jews relocated around the world, still clinging on to many aspects of Spanish culture through the centuries. The current Spanish government, as a way to make amends with the downtrodden community, passed a law that would allow Sephardi Jews to reclaim Spanish nationality.

That much was true.

However, when this news hit the treacherous world of social media, it quickly got conflated with elements that were entirely fabricated. Soon, a list containing Spanish last names (over five thousand of them) that would supposedly qualify for Spanish citizenship started making the rounds. The phony list of unknown origin spread like wildfire among Latin Americans who didn't know any better. Many of them began to draft their futures in Spain, even hiring lawyers to take care of the paperwork.

"*Valencia...*" I repeated. It seemed that now, the barber was cozying up to Spain, mere minutes after adopting a prehispanic indigenous perspective to vilify it. Be that as it may, I was happy to discuss the current Spain I knew and cherished. I injected some trivial information to spur on the conversation.

"Valencia! That's the city paella comes from," I added.

"Yes... Anyway, I may look into it... Los Angeles is a tough city".

"You can say that again!" I agreed.

"I have friends in Spain. They say it's more relaxed over there, no?" he asked as he cut the hairs behind my ear. "*Inclínese un poquito... Ándale.*"

The man's questions probed me in unsuspected ways. Yes, Spain was *relaxing*. The climate, the safety, the cultural offerings... All these things were conducive to enjoying a good *rest*. But the idea of a good rest seemed unearned in an environment where work has hard to come by.

"Spain relaxed? I'd say, for better or for worse..."

"I need some of that. You can't relax much here, too much work! And you can't relax back in Mexico on account of all the violence," he lamented.

"I hear you".

"Who knows what I'll do. I don't quite like it here, but I know I won't go back to Mexico…"

"You'll figure it out", I said. Whereas moments before I was enduring uncomfortable accusations against my nationality, I now found myself fraternizing with a fellow migrant over that same question that liked to haunt me at night: *where is my place in the world?*

6. Mojado.

In the case of thousands of undocumented migrants who are never able to legalize their residence in the U.S., el *desarraigo* packs the potent punch that comes with the devastating understanding that they may never set foot on their motherland again. Their memories become dreams never to be relived. This was yet another way in which I simply could not equate my situation to the frail predicaments of the Hispanic migrants living around me. Although I had also faced my fair share of obstacles relative to being a migrant, they paled in comparison to the plights of the migrants hailing from the south. I arrived in LA by plane and lived a perfectly comfortable life with the law on my side. Although I was indeed prompted by an economic crisis in my home country of Spain, I was by no means escaping a dangerous situation or trying to leave hunger and misery behind. Any time I pleased, I could return home to a nation that was not ravished by violence and corruption. For folks like Luis and Isabel, who had endured an insurmountable journey towards peace and prosperity, a voluntary return to their native lands was simply out of the question.

Nonetheless, I had also met migrants who decided to cut their American Dreams short to return to their homeland. Not long ago, in the state of Guanajuato, México, my wife and I ran out of gas in the middle of a country road. We were taking in the scenery aboard the cheapest rental car we could find and, much to our dismay, we found that the vehicle did not alert the driver with even the slightest beep or dimmest light that the engine would soon be running on fumes. The situation was not desirable in the least, as we were travelling with our five-month-old daughter, about to be stranded in the middle of nowhere. As the car began to stall, we were able to pull up to the side of the road where a homey family restaurant was located, halfway between Dolores Hidalgo and the city of Guanajuato. The place was called Rancho Enmedio, (something like *"Ranch in the way")*. There, we were greeted by a couple in their thirties who ran the place. The wife took care of the cooking while the husband tended to the business side. They had a young daughter, about four years old, and the wife's mother living with them in a small house adjacent to the restaurant. We told them of our mishap on the road and the man, José, agreed to drive me in his car to the nearest place where we could fill a can of gas to take back and resume our trip. My wife and baby stayed put at the restaurant with the women.

On the roads of El Bajío, I spent a good hour with José. In my attempts to make interesting conversation as to make the favor less burdensome for him, I was able to get a pretty good idea of the man's journey. Shy at first, he started to open up after we hit the subject of soccer (*fútbol*). He told me his greatest joy in life, outside of his family, was the amateur league he played with his local friends.

"One lives for those moments", he asserted, declaring he was eager to get back on the pitch after an ankle injury sidelined him for the most recent couple of fixtures. "It's been giving me trouble for years", he lamented. "I hurt it badly when playing in a pickup game *del otro lado*". The expression caught me unaware. *'The other side'.*

"You mean you were on the other team or what?"

"No, I was living *del otro lado*, as a *mojado*," he clarified.

"Oh, I see."

It always struck me as odd how the term *wetback* (*"mojado"*) is such a taboo in the U.S. among English speakers, while the people the term describes, (pejoratively or matter-of-factly), use it so casually when relating their own stories. Most *mojados* I spoke to carried the term proudly like a badge of honor. To proclaim one had been a *mojado* had valiant connotations, like echoes of an intrepid voyage into the unknown. But not all *mojados* were fearless and audacious like Shackleton's men, and many made it to the other side only to end up putting all their troubles and endurances on a tipping scale before concluding that, all things considered, the *mojado* life just wasn't worth it. José was one such man.

"I got tired of that life. They sell you an idea of the States, like it is Heaven on Earth. But once you get there, it's hardly what you've heard in the stories."

Jose's eyes were locked somewhere between the road and the horizon as he reminisced.

"They tell you there's violence here while the U.S. is safe. It's not true. I lived in Chicago, in the areas a *mojado* can afford, and there were muggings and killings every week. They tell you there's poverty here while they U.S. is so rich. It's not true. I saw hundreds of people living in the streets, and some of them froze to death. The truth is, both countries have their good things and their problems, and I'd rather live at home."

José moved through different towns and cities throughout the U.S. and tried to settle various times in a place to call his new home. However, an itch kept gnawing at him in his mind and spirit, urging him to keep looking. There was always some new promising lead, vaguely defined through rumors and half-truths. *"A friend's friend's restaurant is hiring in Wichita"*. *"Detroit needs migrants to revitalize the city"*. *"Cheap land sold in Montana."* *"A distant relative works in the Los Angeles school district, and he could get you a janitor position."* *"The state of Georgia hiring for harvest season"*. Each opportunity seemed slightly better than the last, or so José told himself. And so, the *mojado* nomad kept probing the U.S. geography, east and west of the Mississippi. At one point of his meandering exodus, he started messaging an old high-school sweetheart still living in Guanajuato. Between the two, an old romance was slowly rekindled, and soon José's mind and heart were occupied entirely by his newly found distant love living in his native town. The itch somehow mutated into something different. Whereas before it kept telling him to persist in his search for a new home, now it seemed to certify that his new home would be none other than his old one: Guanajuato. There was no need to keep searching. Now José just needed to relocate there and scratch the itch for good.

"Was it difficult to decide to move back, to stop giving it a shot?" I asked him.

"I thought it would be. I felt maybe my big break in the States was just around the corner and I'd never see it. But once I got back to México, got married, had a baby girl... Well, like they say, there's no place like home."

We arrived in a village called Santa Rosa de Lima, located in the middle of an extensive country road. There were no gas stations, but José knew of some neighbors who sold bootlegged gasoline out of their own houses. After knocking on a couple doors, we were told which house to approach to buy fuel. We found the clandestine gas peddler, and old man living in a shack that was both a crafts workshop and a modest living space. He filled our canister free of charge.

"Enjoy your visit!" he said as he sent José and I on our way.

On the way back to his restaurant, the light turned golden as sunset approached. The fields and sights we passed appeared particularly bucolic as the fresh breeze penetrated the car through the windows. The air was warm and comforting and carried the pleasant smell of May's blossoming flowers.

"You smell that? It's xoconostle season" José said with a smile. The xoconostle, he explained, is a regional prickly pear used extensively in El Bajío's gastronomy. José said he planned a day excursion soon with his family to pick xoconostles in the hills surrounding his home. "It's not always easy! They grow on very spiky *saguaros*…!"

"It sounds fun. I'd love to try one."

As we drove on, the country's aromas were so sweet they overpowered the smell of the gasoline canister tucked between my feet. I told José I perfectly understood why he would want to return home to Mexico. He reasserted his position.

"Look, over there in the States, one can have a ton of things. But really, you don't need most of them to be happy. In fact, people there are never content. They can have anything and everything, but they will always want more. And the more they have, the harder they have to work to afford it all. But here? We keep things simple. We appreciate what we have, and don't lament what we do not have. Because how could we miss what we've never had?"

"So do you think all migrants would be better off if they returned?", I asked him. He paused to consider.

"No, no... I guess speak for myself". He reflected for a few seconds. "The truth is, I've always had it pretty good. I became a *mojado* just to give it a shot. I wanted to see the US, try it for a while. It's not like I was fleeing from danger. But I commend all the *mojados* who have no other option. Trust me, the illegal life is for the very desperate... and the very brave."

7. Maje.

And indeed, it is the brave and desperate who, day in, day out, embark on the uncertain exodus northbound. Some months after Luis and Isabel's caravan arrived at the border, another bigger caravan departed from Honduras. This one managed to stir up larger media turmoil from the get-go, in large part due to the tense images that aired from the Guatemalan border. Scenes of migrants charging through the line of resisting Guatemalan officials did not do the caravan's public perception any favors. After a few days of crossing, the caravan finally arrived in Tijuana, and matters did not improve when some migrants biding their time on the beach decided to sit defiantly on the very fence the separates the two nations. On the American side, just beyond a literal stone's throw from the border, a line of border patrol officers stood, alert and armed to the teeth.

The number of people in this particular caravan was uncertain, but it was easily the largest to date, with media reporting between 5,000 to 8,000 components. The American media spoke of an incoming invasion, while the Tijuana local news seemingly presented the frenzy of a saturated city about to burn to the ground. And yet, on the streets, Tijuanenses carried about the usual business, tangentially keeping up with the news with more curiosity than resent. After all, Tijuana is a city of migrants, and the current migratory episode, although more intense than those in the past, ultimately amounted to yet another wave of hopefuls that may end up becoming part of the city's fabric. Beneath the superficial layer of tabloid journalism, Tijuanenses generally empathized. However, the locals' good will and welcoming demeanor was put to the test when a particular video made the rounds on social media. It featured a Honduran woman with a decidedly entitled attitude speaking ills of the donated food – tortillas and fried beans- and of the charity services in general. This stung the city of Tijuana, which responded with proverbial Mexican sarcasm and outright repudiation. The kneejerk reactions were aimed at the caravan in general, and not at the sole speaker of those unfortunate words.

Tensions reached new heights when a group of migrants broke away from a peaceful protest in the streets of Tijuana and charged for the border. Many carried children, and many managed to permeate the fence and set foot on U.S. soil. They were immediately met with tear gas from border officials. The spontaneous invasion was dead on arrival. Arrests were made on both sides of the fence and deportations swiftly ensued. What really ruffled the Tijuanenses' feather was not so much that the migrants were forfeiting the city's good faith, but that the charge for the border had caused the San Ysidro port of crossing to shut down indefinitely. This was no small inconvenience. It was an immense blow to what makes the city of Tijuana the strategic hub that it is. The shutdown momentarily severed the deeply rooted symbiosis with Tijuana's pretty sister city, San Diego. Earth's busiest land border had unilaterally closed its gates. While all this was going on, I found myself on a train from LA, southbound for San Diego. My final destination was indeed Tijuana, but my family adverted me to avoid crossing until things had quieted down and the port of entry reopened. I killed time in a movie theater in downtown San Diego and approached the border close to midnight. To my amazement, the border was open and eerily quiet. I walked into Tijuana and there were no discernible signs of the earlier incidents of that day. It was a stark contrast with the ongoing news the circulated the web. I decided then and there I needed to visit the caravan to speak to those folks to appreciate the nitty-gritty of the whole phenomenon.

~ ~

The following day I set out in search of the migrants. If guided by the media, one would think they would not be hard to find, as it would seem the city had already succumbed to foreign vagrants. After minimal research, I pinpointed the location of their main shelter: the outdoor sports facility Benito Juarez in Tijuana's city center, pressed right up against the border. I parked in the vicinity and roamed the streets looking for telltale signs of Honduran presence, which quickly manifested itself.

"¡Maje, vos no sabés...!"

Hondurans, for sure; *maje* is Honduran slang for *dude*, and Hondurans use the term *vos* (*you*) instead of the *tú* form favored in most Spanish-speaking countries. I turned to see a group of young men talking and laughing, huddled together to fend off the morning chill. I brought with me with me a large bin liner filled with clothes I'd been meaning to donate for months. I introduced myself and asked if they knew where I could make donations. They kindly pointed me to the donations stand about a hundred yards from where we stood, where about forty migrants waited in line. The small group I was with timidly indicated I could leave the clothes with them.

"The volunteers receive tons of donations at the shelter. We ask when we'll see any of it, and we're always told 'later, later'", they told me. One of them implied that the volunteers were selling the donations somewhere, while another suggested that they needed to keep inventory and triage the needs of the migrants. Be it as it may, one thing was certain; the young men could use my clothes now. It had been raining through the night and the clothes on them were damp. Christian, a slender seventeen-year-old from Tegucigalpa, told me how they could hardly sleep the night before, as the rainfall had dampened the entire dirt soccer field on which they were camping.

"We all woke up in puddles today. It was crazy", the teen chuckled, almost like he was narrating summer camp shenanigans.

I handed over the bin liner, mostly filled with men's shirts and sweaters, and asked them to take the bare minimum each. They went through the contents of the bag swiftly and without wangling. When they were done, it has still half full. One of them procured the bin liner itself, cut holes in the corners, and put in on as a trench coat.

"This is perfect for the rain!" he extolled. They assured me they'd take the rest inside the shelter where more fellow travelers could benefit from clean clothes. A migrant by the name of Samuel, from San Pedro Sula, asked if I had extra socks and underwear. I told him no.

The migrants soon picked up on my Spanish accent and before we knew it we were talking about European soccer -the best icebreaker among Hispanic men. After exchanging passionate opinions about the beautiful game, the migrants started to tell me their own stories. Not much had changed from those of the previous caravan: violence, corruption, extortion, and a lack of opportunities had driven them out of their land by the thousands. Eloel, who went by Elvis, had a prominent scar on his cheek from his encounter with the bloodthirsty *salvatruchas*. The next time, they assured him, he wouldn't live to tell the tale.

Bulnes, from San Pedro Sula, still carried a bullet buried in his thigh, courtesy of –you guessed it- gang members. He told me that medical attention in Honduras is so precarious that when he rushed to the hospital with a fresh bullet wound, the doctor said he'd need to be paid up front before proceeding to amputate his leg, alleging the entire limb was beyond repair. Asking the patients to finance their own surgeries is not uncommon, as social security funds in Honduras systematically fall in the hands of corrupt governors. It behooves patients to bring their own gauze pads and ethanol to ensure the most sanitary procedure. As luck would have it, Bulnes could not round up the funds and the day after he was introduced to an American volunteer surgeon. Not only did the American tend to Bulnes free of charge, but also he was able to salvage the extremity with no apparent sequels other than the lead artifact still being lodged deep in his thigh.

"And your leg's fine and dandy now?!" I asked him.

"Well, here I am, after a very long walk!" he said with a big smile, his arms outstretched exuding pride in his feat.

I heard several testimonies from the migrants. There was Olman, a young Nicaraguan who joined the caravan in Honduras after escaping the political killings in his home country. There was Chapulín, the one with the bin liner on, who must have been in his late fifties. He was the eldest of the group and went by that name because he fancied himself a doppelganger of the famous Mexican TV character. The resemblance was dubious at best, but I wouldn't be the one to tell him that. José David and Wilson, two migrants from Copán, sported bright orange vests, given to them at the construction gig they landed the day before. They were not currently working but wore their uniforms in their downtime all the same. For the rest of the group, they were an identifier of prosperity, a silver lining in a circumstance of sheer apprehension. Christian pointed to them in awe.

"Look, they already found *chamba!*" he exclaimed, genuinely happy for them.

I asked each of them what their plans were, and was surprised to see that, in many cases, seeking political asylum in the U.S. had fallen out of preference. A few of them were willing to give Tijuana a chance. Its blooming infrastructure meant there was plenty of work to be found in construction, a field that many of the migrants were proficient in. Some others were particularly excited about seeking asylum in other countries, such as Chile, Brazil, Canada and Spain. Various charity organizations from these countries had flown to Tijuana to explain to the migrants how their chances of landing humanitarian visas improved significantly in those far away nations. Although the volunteers made convincing cases, they could not sway the many migrants whose sights were solely set on the U.S., as they already had family waiting there. Among these migrants, there were a few who planned to hitch rides east of the small border town of Tecate, about thirty miles from Tijuana. They had heard that it's easier to breach the much less sentineled fence over there in the inhospitable Sonoran Desert.

"So what about asylum in the States? What about doing it by the book?" I inquired.

"Man, I don't know. We don't like our chances. Those idiots that jumped the fence the other day really did a number on us." Samuel replied.

I pointed out the incoherence in his words, and he was quick to get on the defensive.

"It's one thing to climb over the border in large numbers all at once, defiantly, using children as shields, throwing rocks at the patrol. If I cross, I'll make sure I don't bother anybody. Is it even an invasion if nobody even knows you're there?" he posed.

Samuel was adamant to split hairs, and I didn't have it in me to tell him I didn't think his reasoning was airtight. It was evident to me that the migrants drew clear distinctions between the concepts of illegality and immorality. While a lot of them had no problem with the idea of crossing the border illegally in order to live an otherwise wholesome life, they did have qualms with some of the troublemakers that came in the caravan. As we spoke, one of the migrants lit up a pocket-sized bong, sat down on the sidewalk, and proceeded to smoke up. Upon seeing this, the group distanced itself from the smoker.

"Amigos, that guy is not helping your case," I told them.

"We know that..." Samuel sighed. "We don't want to be associated with that kind of behavior. If the police show up and we're with him, they'll round us all up. They don't really care whodunit. *Aquí pagamos justos por pecadores*", he explained. *The innocent pay for the the sins of the guilty.*

"We've put up with a lot", Bulnes lamented. "The damn woman who doesn't like frijoles, the *locos* that charged over the fence, the idiots making a mess in the streets... The media is right about one thing: not everybody in this caravan is an *angelito*..."

They told me how they had begun to report wrongdoing to the authorities. They had already turned in various migrants who were caught stealing from the others. It was hardly petty theft, as the few possessions the migrants carried were all they had in this world. The Tijuana police apprehended the thieves and set them up for deportation. However, not all migrants were willing to take part in the weeding out of the caravan, as they still carried with them the daunted mantra that was typical in the tougher barrios of Honduras. *"See nothing, say nothing"*. For many, this philosophy had meant the difference between life and death.

After a long conversation, I treated the migrants to coffee from the 7-Eleven down the block.

"It's not Honduran coffee, but hey, it will keep you warm and awake", I excused myself. They laughed.

"No, this is great. Thank you so much."

As we sipped our cheap java, they let me take their photograph. They nestled closely for the camera while I stepped back and readied my lens. I looked up again and noticed the group had multiplied by three. I got it; *this nosey Spaniard buys you coffee if you let him take your photo.* I snapped a few shots and indeed gave in to my absurd predicament, obliging the newcomers with more 7-Eleven Americano. As I handed them the warm cardboard cups, an unkempt old man with a scruffy beard and pungent odor pushed through the crowd and grabbed the first one.

"Hey!! Don't give him one! He's not with us!" cried Christian, worried that one of the migrants would not get his due coffee.

"Wait, wasn't he in the photo with you just now?" I asked, baffled.

"He snuck in. He's not with us! He's a homeless man!" the teen testified, snatching the coffee from the old man's hands.

"And what are we, *maje*?" challenged Bulnes calmly. He handed his own coffee to the old man. The intruder took it and, without uttering a word, wandered off into the streets of Tijuana.

The group walked me to the actual campsite, located five blocks away. It was on Calle 5 de Mayo, a cul-de-sac that ended, along with the entire nation, on the international border fence itself. The campsite was filled with tents, tarps, mats, sleeping bags, and had a few portable restrooms on one side of the street. The long lines outside clearly indicated that there were not enough toilets for the thousands of migrants. A banner hanging from one of the tents read: *"We are not criminals. We are international workers"*.

The campsite was visibly more disorganized that the one I visited some months before, and I quickly learned why. Local authorities were in the process of relocating the thousands of migrants to another area far from downtown Tijuana, where they would not disrupt the city center's daily operations and where they could be granted better sanitary attention. Much had been made of the migrants' health, or lack thereof. Many journalists on the site wore antiviral facemasks and chose long lenses to photograph the migrants from a considerable distance. News on both sides of the border had described the campsite as a cesspool of disease. I raised this issue with one of the Red Cross volunteers. He dismissed the morbid headlines.

"There have been many cases of hair lice and colds, which is to be expected. We have located a handful of cases of chickenpox, which can spread fast through children and potentially cause pneumonia on unimmunized adults. So no, they're not zombies, but we have to keep potential outbreaks at bay", he said, adding that vaccines had been dished out diligently from the first day. He stressed the importance of moving the migrants somewhere with more space, as overcrowding could be conducive to the rise of more serious infections.

The migrants, on the other hand, were not too keen to move. Many of them had found odd jobs in Tijuana's effervescent center. With all of them lacking their own transportation, they could not afford to be moved miles away from the hustle and bustle of *el centro,* and the opportunities it presented. The city had provided buses to make the trip to the next campsite, and many migrants were happy to get onboard. Others, however, wouldn't budge, yelling: "We're not moving! We have jobs here now!" Of course, this argument meant little to local authorities, as whatever jobs the migrants may have found were little more than trivial chores for local merchants, and strictly speaking, they were working illegally. But to those migrants, without a dime to their name, those jobs meant the world. They were starting to get ahead, but authorities that claimed to want the best for them were nullifying their progress. As volunteers stripped the campsite down, a few migrants stayed anchored, guarding their tents with unflinching conviction. The tension was palpable. Of course, it was the officials who would get the upper hand. The migrants could do nothing but watch as the trump card was coldly laid on the table; a large crane truck arrived and, in a matter of minutes, hoisted up the mobile toilets and showers and swiftly took them away. *Checkmate.*

Discussions broke out among those who wanted to stay. Now their position wasn't so certain, as they knew that if they insisted on staying behind, the public perception of them would no longer be that they're refugees, but mere indigent vagrants engrossing the homeless population of the run-down city center.

As the camp disintegrated, many migrants dispersed into the city center, hell-bent on carving their own fates without the need for the altruism of third parties. It wasn't that they were ungrateful to the charities, volunteers, and federal assistance that had aided them so much since their arrival. But depending solely on charity implied abiding always to their terms. *Sleep here. Eat this. Don't go there. Get in line.* Many migrants, particularly men, felt ready to fly the nest and emancipate from the tightly ordained precepts that presided over the campsite. Jason, a native of Colón, Honduras, was feeling pretty good about his newly found job as an unloader at the Mercado Hidalgo. His next goal was to find a cheap room for rent to call his new home.

"I unload tons and tons of coconuts a day. I deserve a proper bed to crash for the night!" he sighed with a weary smile.

I caught up with him as he took a turn for one of Tijuana's most infamous streets, La Coahuila. He'd been told he was liable to find lodging there, and to a degree, that was true. However, I averted him to try to avoid La Coahuila if possible, as it was known to be one of Tijuana's seediest areas. It wasn't just a red-light district. Gun violence would often break out in La Coahuila and the streets and alleys that stemmed from it. Drunken brawls escalating into shootouts, drug bosses settling scores on unsuspecting foes while they were being tended to in brothels, lost tourists getting mugged by junkie drifters... Conflict came in all flavors in La Coahuila, a street with a proverbially short fuse. Even though Jason could sense the street's disreputable fame in the air, he was lured by the comparatively low prices he was seeing on the rooms for rent.

"Jason, look elsewhere" I encouraged him. "You left Honduras to leave trouble behind", I reminded him. "This part of town is *nothing* but trouble."

"But look at those prices", he said pointing to the sign of a hostel behind me. "150 pesos a night. I can afford that!" I turned to face the hostel.

"It's 150 pesos for two hours, Jason. Those beds are not for sleeping...!" I told him. Jason was visibly discouraged but determined to find something. We parted ways as he went on exploring the city.

8. Playas.

That afternoon, I headed for Playas de Tijuana, the city's coastal area. Playas, as it was simply known among the locals, had a slightly different bearing than the rest of the city. It was considerably less hectic and felt somewhat left behind in the Tijuana's infrastructural renaissance. With the bullfighting arena and beach as the main attractions, Playas was particularly picturesque, albeit not without its sordidly dilapidated spots. The sunsets over the Pacific were beautiful, in stark contrast with the sights that hypnotic golden light came to rest upon.

An up-and-coming boardwalk area bordered wonky and decrepit apartment buildings. The walk featured a few impoverished businesses and a timid slew of modern venues, such as gourmet coffee shops and hookah bars. These alternated with run-down houses and seafood stands the likes of which attracted tourists with their prices and then sent them to ride the *thunder bucket* for days. This was the reaction many foreigners had to local foods and constituted yet another reason why many potential visitors would avoid traveling to the city of Tijuana –or Mexico altogether. The locals, on the other hand, were immune to Moctezuma's revenge, -as they liked to call a tourist's food poisoning in México. Tijuanenses loved to see the days out by watching the sun dip behind the ocean while sipping their beloved micheladas and clamatos.

On a clear day on Playas de Tijuana, it was possible to see the city of San Diego some twenty miles away, its skyline gleaming in the distance with splendorous dignity. The office buildings and luxury apartments reached for the sky, as did the majestic Coronado Bridge, high enough for aircraft carriers to sail beneath it. The imposing structure rose and descended with grace, connecting downtown San Diego with the affluent peninsula of Coronado. Even from miles away, San Diego looked stately and impressive, but without pretense. It appeared in the distance the way it is, nothing less and nothing more. Tijuana, with all of its troubles and colorful idiosyncrasies, peered at its well-to-do neighbor from afar, split between developing a complex and standing up with pride in being so one-of-a-kind. *"Aquí empieza la patria"*. Tijuana was far from the orderly city San Diego is, but it had an edgy character that almost made San Diego appear dull. Pristine, but dull.

One thing was clear: most Sandiegans didn't return this longing gaze. Many, in fact, preferred to live as if Tijuana did not exist. For them, the world extended North and East only. There was nothing worthwhile going South. Years of drug-related violence had deterred Americans from crossing to Tijuana, and even though the carnage had decreased significantly in the past decade, Tijuana still carried the crucible of being a synonym of *danger* in the minds of the cautious gringos. There were, however, a few niche U.S. communities that appreciated Tijuana and made the most of its proximity. The Chicanos of San Diego would visit their motherland frequently with itineraries such as: *visit the dentist, visit the mechanic, go eat tacos.*

Chicanos were not the only ones to visit the border city in large numbers from the north. In playas, it was not uncommon to find entire families of Amish and Mennonites from the Midwest visiting Tijuana for its cheap and reliable medical services. Said religions don't allow their parishioners to have medical insurance, as it is seen as a form of gambling. Paying the exorbitant doctor bills out of pocket in the U.S. was out of the question. Curiously, Tijuana provided a solution to the plight of these communities. Not a perfect solution, as they would have to ride the train for days all the way from the Mid-West to San Diego (air travel is also prohibited). But it was a solution nonetheless. It was common for them to put off procedures, bordering on negligence, until the entire family had motives to go to Tijuana in order to make the trip a worthy investment for all involved. Amish and Mennonite families were a common sight in Playas, where they enjoyed walking on the shore and taking in the sea breeze that was so foreign in their landlocked communities. My first sighting of Amish people in Tijuana was akin to an apparition. I had read about their reserved and simple way of life, and I simply couldn't believe they'd wander so far from home. But they had their reasons for being in Tijuana, as did I. Reasons that weren't obvious but were reasons all the same. As they strolled on the beach barefooted, their spoken Pennsylvania Dutch graced the ambience and mixed with the *rancheras* playing on local radio, creating an eccentric scene that could well have come from some outlandish dream. They always moved in groups in this uncharted territory, and the sight of San Diego in the distance provided some comfort. After all, the modern and stylish Californian city was still very much at odds with their quaint and anachronistic lifestyle. But still, San Diego was one realm closer to home.

For the stranded and forsaken souls of Tijuana, the sight of San Diego might as well have been a glimpse of Mount Olympus, a divine place they'd never experience up close. Playas de Tijuana was *finis terrae*. The end of the line. This harsh fact was perfectly epitomized in the border fence that extended from hundreds of miles away, ran across the sandy beach and stretched out into the ocean, completing the split of North America in two. The fence itself had more symbolic weight than real material effectiveness. It was made of tall slabs of rusty metal, interconnected with rather prosaic metal mesh. Any decent climber would have no trouble rising to the top of the structure, -as some Honduran migrants had done in the days prior-, but this part of the border was always heavily guarded from the other side. In fact, in the light of recent events, when I showed up, more layers of barbed wire were being installed on the American side. Sure, one could climb onto the fence from Mexico, but would you really want to come down on gringo territory? If the deadly curls of razor-sharp metal weren't enough to dissuade you, maybe the armed border patrol's piercing international stare would do the trick. They were always watching the lively occurrences of Playas, and should anybody decide to invade the neighbor's home, the patrol's trigger fingers were always ready to observe the time-honored Second Amendment.

Of course, nobody on either side of the fence wanted such a scene to ever come to pass. On the Mexican side, a coastguard SUV remained parked on the beach about twenty yards from the fence. They weren't there so much to treat stingray stings or warn against rip currents, but rather to prevent any curious beachgoer from swimming along the fence all the way to its end and peek around, and even -God forbid- try to swim to the U.S. shore. Chances are they wouldn't be met with a towel, but rather find themselves staring down the business end of a rifle.

That afternoon, I saw the Mexican coastguard spring to action when a Honduran migrant with a few too many drinks on him started to walk into the sea. He had been taunting the border patrol on the other side for some time, and his provocative intentions were clear. He held onto the international fence as the choppy waterline rose on him, his sight set firmly on the end of the border. The coastguard sounded the SUV's siren to no effect. Border patrol on the other side observed calmly, not too content with the idea of having to deal with a trespasser. The migrant seemed to be out of his depth, yet slowly but surely progressed toward the end of the fence. The coastguard finally ran into the water, caught up to him and gently tugged him away from the fence. They split through the water obliquely and arrived onshore about ten yards from the border. The migrant looked back through the fence defiantly. He was clearly inebriated.

"Am I not allowed to go for a fucking swim? What were you gonna do, *comemierdas*?" he jeered at the agents, who looked on impassively. It would appear that such episodes were not an uncommon occurrence. The whole incident took place in front of a crowd of beachgoers, migrants, and journalists who watched on pins and needles. When it was over, a few jokes were made to ease the tension in the air. A Mexican hawker selling corncobs and shrimp skewers approached the fence to address the agents and workers who were setting up the additional barbed wire.

"Don't mind that idiot, he's drunk! Here, why don't you buy one of these delicious treats?", he said as he poked a skewer through the fence's mesh. His proposition was ignored. "Don't worry!" he added, "I don't charge extra for international shipping! But I will take dollars and dollars only". His joke was met with laughter on the Mexican side only. Whether the Americans didn't understand Spanish, or simply were not in a laughing mood remained unclear. They observed unflinchingly, never reacting to any of the conversations or provocations coming from the Mexican side. The border patrol wore camouflage, body-armor, sunglasses, and carried heavy firearms. This imposing attire along with their sturdy and impassive presence made it easy to stop seeing them as people, and rather start thinking of them as callous and lethargic sentinels submitted to a higher power. For this reason, it was a delightful treat to catch a glimpse of their humanity, however small and fleeting.

"*Cuidado, ola!*", said a border patrol agent with a thick American accent, projecting his voice timidly through the fence. "*Careful, wave*". He was clearly addressing the Mexicans, who were caught unaware of an incoming wave that washed ashore with unrestrained momentum. It would have reached the feet of many present on the Mexican side were it not for the border agent's notice. As the wave rolled back into the sea on both sides of the fence, the Mexicans erupted in applause, a celebration that was not without a healthy dose of sarcasm.

"*¡Nos salvaste del chaparrón! ¡Nuestro héroe!*" the migrants teased. To everyone's surprise, the border agent responded with a quick smirk. "He smiled!! Finally!" said the migrants in genuine merriment.

With the sun almost gone, the migrants shortly began to make the trip back to wherever it was they would be spending the night. Another day drew to a close in the city of Tijuana. Another day of the city's unsuspected embrace around a vastly disparate amalgam of travelers and settlers, -and the odd travelers who had settled but didn't know it yet. The stars appeared to glimmer over them all: the Tijuanenses that went back many generations, the newcomers from inland México, the hopeful Honduran migrants looking for a fighting chance, the affable Haitians who were already making the most of that chance, the gringo tourists that visited in perfectly calculated incursions, the well-to-do locals with blue passports who spent their lives betting on two horses, the Amish and the Mennonites getting a taste for modernity in a far-off land, and one lone Spaniard trying to make sense of it all. In the distance, a seagull flew high over the border fence and into Mexican territory. Untethered by centuries of geopolitical differences, uninterrupted by the border patrol far below, the seagull chose to land gracefully on the beach of Tijuana. She looked around at the scene around her, and I wondered if she could tell the difference from her previous stop in gringo land. She squawked a couple times before resuming her flight south. *"De este lado también hay sueños"*. Maybe so.

PART TWO

A very real imaginary line

1. La Línea.

For many years now –most would say since the infamous date of September 11th, 2001- a modern and robust border culture had been established at the Mexico-U.S. ports of entry. It was rigid, unforgiving, tenacious, and mechanized with cutting-edge security hardware and the latest in ID technology. The process had become dense, airtight, and thorough –a far cry from what it had been before the aforementioned date, a date that changed borders all around the world forever. Stories circulated by old-timers told of a long-gone era in which the lines to cross were hardly lines at all. An era in which you could waltz into the U.S. without as much as flashing your ID card, your entry based solely on the merit of *looking* somewhat American. If you could, in passing, say a couple words in perfect English, then you'd be met with a friendly smile. *Welcome back.*

I've even heard from people who, in their youth, would mount their bicycles and speed through the border booths, not pressing the brakes once, to go from Mexicali, (Mexico) to Calexico (U.S.). Back then, it seemed, children were beyond any shadow of a doubt. Now, when we cross, my toddler daughter's booster seat is routinely inspected for cocaine, firearms, explosives, –what have you!

"Don't pet the dog, *hija.*" I tell her when the K9 unit approaches. "Not this one".

The San Ysidro port of entry is a sight to behold, and perhaps, unofficially, the most iconic landmark in Tijuana. It's not necessarily beautiful by any standards, but it is impressive. The bumper-to-bumper traffic extending as far as the eye can see, the endless waits, the flood lights, the barbed wire, the cameras, the police dogs, the fire breathers (more on those later...) It all makes for an intense, almost harrowing experience, one compounded by the poetic significance of this particular border. The elicited emotions, however intense, made every bit of sense. You truly *felt* you were in the divide between thirty-something countries of the developing world and the globe's most important and influential nation. You truly *felt* you were at the frontier between a land governed by corruption and cartel violence and a nation that proclaimed law and order with its implacable legal institutions. You truly *felt* you were leaving a land of baroquely colorful heritage, filled with wonder and passion, and entering a country marked by its acutely practical, overly materialistic, and almost aseptic take on life. Many of the peddlers and entertainers who made a living in the vicinity of the border would never get to know the other side. For them, that reality existed only in their collective imagination. It wasn't just a border; it was the last fringe of their known reality. It felt like a portal into another dimension, one where things became foreign and mystifying to a point of stupor. Beyond the border lay the fascinating unknown. It's all too fitting that the Spanish word for border and frontier is the same: *frontera*.

At its peak when the traffic is busiest, there are about twenty lines of cars patiently awaiting entry into the U.S. The lines during rush hour can extend for a few kilometers and cause serious traffic in other distant areas of the city. This line (simply known as *"la línea"* in Tijuana lingo) is one of the most influential factors in everyday life at the border. People live by it, organizing their days around when it is busiest and when it's quietest.

There are really three lines; the SENTRI, the Ready Lane, and the normal line. Being able to use one or the other can amount to huge differences in overall quality of living. This constitutes something like Tijuana's very own theory of relativity. A commonly held belief about this city, if tongue-in-cheek, is that the best part of it living in Tijuana is San Diego. That is to say, the best aspect of life in Tijuana has really little or nothing to do with Tijuana itself. It is the Californian city of San Diego (regarded as one of the best cities to live in across the entire U.S. territory) that really gives its neighbor, Tijuana, an edge over other Mexican cities that have more to show for themselves. In this sense, how easily one can make the trip from Tijuana to San Diego directly affects Tijuana's quality of life –or lack thereof. The three different lines used to cross relate time and space in vastly varying ways, warping these planes of reality not unlike Einstein poised in his famous postulate. The most fortunate travelers can cover this distance in a reasonable time, almost as if there was no border to speak of at all. For others, the drive from Tijuana to San Diego is equivalent to the drive between Paris and Brussels –that is, about four hours. For the less fortunate, the time spent in line would be sufficient to cover the distance between Marseille in Southern France to Rome, Italy (seven hours by car). The proverbial *"so close, yet so far"* certainly applies here.

The SENTRI line (Secure Electronic Network for Travelers Rapid Inspection) advances the fastest and, since arriving at the border, it usually takes SENTRI travelers less than ten minutes to drive into the U.S. Anyone could apply for the SENTRI program, but it too was an expensive and slow process that entailed an extenuating background check. The SENTRI pass, if you were fortunate to have it, was among your most valuable assets in Tijuana. It facilitated trips to San Diego, opening up a world of possibilities such as sending the children to school in the U.S., and doing grocery shopping and other errands there (the States generally had *more things*, and this abundance meant many products were in fact significantly cheaper in the U.S. than in Mexico). SENTRI passes, hard as they are to obtain, are in turn easy to revoke. I've met people who had theirs rescinded because of a pleasure trip to Cuba, or because a distant relative living in the U.S. was involved in tax evasion. In the face of information like that, border authorities don't beat around the bush and often resolve in nipping the problem -if there even is one- at the bud. Appeals could be made but were mostly futile; border authorities didn't have time to feel bad for unfairly invalidating a SENTRI pass. After all, the SENTRI status was not a right to be claimed; it was a privilege. If you had it, you were lucky. If it got taken away, you were unlucky. Fairness had nothing to do with it.

The next best thing was the Ready Lane, conceived to make U.S. nationals' reentry into their country less of a tedious ordeal. Essentially, it was a line reserved for people who held American-issued ID's, to provide them with a degree of preference and comfort a nudge higher than that of non-American travelers.

And then there was the normal lane, so normal it didn't have some catchy border nickname. This was the worst line to endure –and the only one I had access to. On a good day, at a very good time (from late night to the wee hours of the morning), it could take around one to two hours to complete. On a bad day, it could run for over seven hours. Your car became your entire living space for that time, as the traffic slowly dragged forward one inch at a time. You don't show up to this line without a carefully devised plan, and people know they would better bring with them some form of entertainment (a book, a film to watch on the smartphone...) or some way of being productive. Being able to do substantial amounts of work on one's cellphone thus becomes a saving grace in this undesirable circumstance.

If crossing alone, you will not be able to use the bathroom for that entire time –for who is going to move your car while you're relieving yourself? If accompanied, getting out of the car and walking to a nearby WC is perfectly feasible. It will cost you ten pesos a pop, or about fifty American cents, and that includes a short ream of toilet paper. It's a very small price to pay for the many unfortunate souls who find themselves stuck in their car when their digestive systems start to wage war against those dubiously cheap street tacos enjoyed a few hours prior; not all street food is to be trusted, even if it's one of Tijuana's greatest claims to fame. This is a maxim to live by in this city, and one should not let their guard down at *la línea*, even after tolerating hours of wait and falling prey to the thought that, maybe, you've earned a tasty treat –perhaps one from the many peddlers patiently ambling amidst the traffic. In this predicament, freshly fried churros are always a good bet. They may not be the best churros you'll ever eat, but they're filling, and chances are you won't get food poisoning from them. Burritos and *tortas* (Mexican hoagies) are risky territory, while the hard-no's go to the seafood cocktails and the *tejuinos* (something like a shaved ice drink derived from an ancient

79

Tarahumara beverage of fermented corn). Don't try these –not in *la línea.*

The many food offerings constitute only a fraction of what can be purchased at *la línea*, where there is a vibrant array of souvenirs not unlike what you would find at an airport. Did you forget to buy a memento for your significant other? The sellers of *la línea* have your back. Ponchos, crucifixes, salsa bowls, maracas and other stereotypically Mexican objects are everywhere. Kitsch art is also a thriving market niche in *la línea.* If you ever wanted a painted evocation of Al Pacino as Scarface sitting at the poker table with real-life Mexican drug kingpin El Chapo, this is the place to acquire just that. Other popular characters such as Frida, Selena, Speedy Gonzalez and Pancho Villa are also present, their likeness stamped on endless items of merchandising. At *la línea*, it becomes perfectly apparent that Mexican culture and what Americans regard as Mexican culture are two very different things. Ever the pragmatists, Mexican sellers are willing to accommodate, even if it meant cozying up to a shallow and almost cartoony reduction of their world. I recall how, in my first visit to Mexico, I too was hell-bent on finding a poncho like the one Clint Eastwood sports in the Dollar Trilogy. I nagged my Mexican friend to guide me to where I could buy one in San Cristóbal de las Casas, Chiapas.

"I hate to break it to you but... You probably won't find a poncho. Ponchos are not really Mexican", she said with a tone that reminded me of a mother telling her child Santa is not real. "Neither are maracas, nor nachos."

However, the sellers at *la línea* are happy to keep the illusion alive, perpetuating a falsehood that rang more and more true as time went by. After all, repeat a lie a thousand times and it becomes the truth, -and the gringos looking for the typically Mexican ponchos and maracas became a self-fulfilling prophecy.

Aside from the food and the paraphernalia, the wait time at *la línea* is made more tolerable by entertainers of all sorts. Duos of street musicians singing *rancheras* in harmony, regional dancers exploiting the twirly skirt cliché, jugglers, acrobats and fire-eaters... They all competed for the attention of the drivers, a tough crowd that became increasingly uninterested in the goings-on outside their vehicles. Instead, they had their eyes firmly locked on their phone-screens as they chatted away or watched a film. I admit I would do this too. Sometimes, upon raising my head, the reality outside my car beat the fiction in my phone screen.

A guy is drinking gasoline and casting fireballs from his mouth.

A man wearing a long gabardine is tapping on my window, trying to sell me puppies –the poor, live animals stuffed in his inner pockets.

A double amputee, resting his stumps on those old-timey crutches, is staggering through the traffic, asking for change.

A child, no older than seven, is juggling balls with mechanical frenzy. Then he meanders through the cars, also looking for alms.

At times, *la línea* did feel like watching a movie; it was over two hours of sitting still as events unfolded before your eyes and strange characters passed you by. Sometimes it was entertaining. Sometimes it was heartbreaking.

In a sense, *la línea* was the perfect spot to put on a show because the many American travelers who had visited Tijuana for the day were more than happy to get rid of the spare pesos they had that would be worthless stateside. There truly wasn't much to do in *la línea,* but you could make these small donations. Sometimes you made them out of sheer pity, sometimes as a truly earned reward for the entertainer, but always as a practical decision to rid your wallet of minted deadweight.

Despite the static and tiresome nature of your typical wait in *la línea,* there was always a sense of restlessness that never quite subsided. The place keeps you on edge. If suddenly the traffic ahead of you progresses a few yards and you're distracted on your phone, a vehicle from an adjacent lane will swerve and plunge into the resulting gap, almost as if sucked by a vacuum. These shameless opportunists are labeled *gaviotas,* (seagulls) and they're the reason the cars at *la línea* leave a space of mere centimeters between one another. Thus, peddlers with big carts often have little to no space to move around, and one has to keep an eye out for the odd mobile churro stand liable to scratch your paintjob. But this is hardly the reason why at *la línea* you commonly find your gaze darting from one rearview mirror to the other. We've all heard of the other familiar threat in some shape or form.

"Keep your wits about you. Don't get distracted. You don't want to get caught smuggling drugs across the border," you would hear.

I don't think it's common. But I *know* it has happened. While you're sitting at the wheel, minding your own business, a pedestrian outside adheres something to your vehicle's underside. It can happen in less than two seconds, while you watch reruns of your favorite episodes on your streaming app. A tiny parcel, tightly wound, is suddenly and firmly stuck to your car. The contents? Colombian cocaine and a GPS tracker. The idea is that you, the well-to-do civilian with the clean record, become the drug smuggler without even knowing it. On the other side of the border, somebody will locate your parked car as you run your errands, minding your business. They pick up the cargo. And you'll go about your life none the wiser. It is perhaps one of the most brilliant (and most vile) innovations in the drug trade; the hardest part of the distribution process –that is, getting the goods into U.S. territory- is delegated to a third party who assumes the greatest risk, and does it for free too... because they don't know they're doing it. These stories circulate the border grapevine as scary cautionary tales, and though they appear distant and almost too cinematic to believe, I've been assured by border officials themselves that said episodes are not that uncommon. By that, of course, they mean that it's not that uncommon that they catch the inadvertent smugglers. But what about all the ones they don't catch? What's the real tally there? And have I ever been one of them in my many border crossings?

2. The Man.

Even though for thousands of people the crossing of said border is an act they routinely carry out, there is always a sense of uneasiness when approaching the officials who receive your documents. When reaching into your pocket or purse, there's always that split second in which you think, maybe, without you realizing, you dropped your passport. Or worse! Maybe somebody pickpocketed you. Your mind even flashes a list of suspects, people who were around you in the long waiting line -this scare is more common when crossing on foot. Pedestrians of all sorts traverse these ports of entry, and often the type of activities they've been involved in while in Tijuana are rather of the disreputable kind. There are the dive bars, the cheap brothels, the casinos with rampant sports betting, and the endless pharmacies that sell drugs that are entirely illegal a few miles north. Tijuana is, after all, a good caterer of vice. I've seen people who reach the border officials utterly intoxicated. It's not unusual to witness these poor fellows flash their ID's at the booth, and stagger away ahead of you, only to find them again in the street stateside, lying on some bench in the sun, engrossing California's ever-growing homeless population. It's a sad phenomenon, and one that's all too common. Unfortunately, these are the folks that keep you alert while waiting in line, and the unconscious go-to explanation when we fear –if only for a fleeting moment- that our ID has been stolen.

But then your fingertips finally feel the worn-out leather fringes of your most treasured document, and you breathe a sigh of relief. The anxiety, however, does not subside entirely. In fact, I find I'm most nervous when my passport is in the hands of the official. What if, through some Kafkaesque turn of events, he ends up retaining my passport and sending me to the proverbial *cuartito* (*the little room*)? This is when a growing sense of paranoia really sets in, precisely as the agent cross-examines the passport and the information on his computer monitor. These machines have a privacy screen filter to make it impossible to read anything on them from an angle. And don't you dare try to position yourself better so you can snoop at the screen! Such small gestures could carry enormous significance for the border official. *Why is he trying to read the screen? Is there something he wishes to hide from us? Is he nervous because our records might have some dirt on him?*

As the official tries to project some guilt-ridden meaning onto every nuance of your body language, you too begin to wonder what exactly they know about you. *Just what is showing up on his screen? Do they have my tax returns? Do they know about that time I ran a red light by accident? Just how centralized is my information? Does DMV provide the border agents with my records? What about the IRS? What about non-American institutions? That time the Spanish police took me for questioning when I was sixteen... Do they know about that too?*

You fear the System. The State. The Man. The Big Brother. The opaque, amorphous amalgam of power, at once ethereal and ironfisted, an authority with information that extends far beyond what we can begin to imagine. There is no doubt in me that the officials, should they wish to, could obtain years of detailed data on me, and not just on my history pertaining to my travels to the U.S. But ultimately, I assured myself I had nothing to worry about. If I had a clear conscience, why would I allow such paranoid thoughts to brew now? Well, there was a bit of a reason. My profile was that of a strange outlier in Tijuana, a quirky oddity that could easily inspire further questions; a Spanish national living in Tijuana with an American 01-B work visa. Oh yes, I'd finally attained this valued legal permit. It had taken years of expensive and sluggishly tedious paperwork, but USCIS finally deemed me a valuable addition to the fabric of the U.S. It would have been a feat worth celebrating if it weren't for the fact that my wife's work visa, filed at the same time as mine, had been rejected. This was a low blow for the two of us, particularly because we both felt her case was stronger. Such is the cold arbitrariness of the whole process. I wasn't about to move to the U.S. by myself, so for now I made the most of my visa while living in Tijuana, as my wife and her immigration lawyers attempted to file her petition case once more. And I didn't have *any* visa. I helmed the 0-1B, that is, the work visa for *"aliens with extraordinary abilities"*. It's a bit of a black belt in the world of U.S. visas. It's the same type of visa foreign Hollywood stars are made to get, so it stands to reason that when border agents saw me drive up in my beat-up Jetta to show them my sumptuous work permit, they usually had some questions.

"Why were you in Tijuana?"

"I live there."

"What do you do for a living?"

"I'm a video producer."

"What types of videos?"

"Digital video."

I had learned to concede the next degree of concretion while at the same time remaining somewhat vague in my replies.

Over my many entries, I'd found the more information you give, the more questions you're asked in return. The name of the game is to be succinct without coming across as cagey, -a difficult balance only attained through endless incursions and practice! Once again, I had nothing to hide. I simply wanted to get through fast, and sometimes responses that were short and sweet fared better than long-winded ones, as these were more conducive to a suspicious stutter, or a Freudian slip, or a perceived *plot-hole* in your purported intentions.

The official flicks through your document, making sense of the different stamps –when you came last, when you left last-, finding your past visas, your current one, finding any exotic stamps that may elicit further questions.

"Why did you go to Turkey?" officials would often ask me sternly, inspecting a five-year-old stamp from Istanbul.

"My honeymoon," I replied.

Some people, in their attempts to seem particularly forthcoming, would give them a more colorful, chit-chatty response. I had always been of the thought that such responses could be interpreted as calculated, devious –a narrative constructed to gloss over or circumvent information one would be unwilling to admit, almost as if trying to cover up some apparent inconsistency the agent may not even have caught yet.

International stamps from exotic destinations were of particular interest to border officials. In my case, I was often asked about my trip to Turkey and several visits to Panama –a nation notorious for being a tax haven and a money-laundering hub for Latin America's biggest drug lords. My wife, who held dual citizenship (Honduran and French), always made a point to receive the more problematic stamps in her Honduran passport and leave a nice clean French passport for the almost exclusive use of U.S. border officials. Sadly, a Honduran passport in and of itself would draw out the interrogation –particularly in the wake of the migrant caravan crisis. The U.S. ports of entry were a place in which it paid to be aware of national stereotypes and connotations, even if these bordered on xenophobic thinking and racial profiling. Being aware and making any necessary adjustments -such as identifying as French as opposed to Honduran- became a matter of practicality.

I would be remiss if I didn't point out that not all border officials were out to get you. Most of them didn't go out of their way to look for red flags. Some were even perfectly helpful and friendly. But the lore, the general sentiment at the ports of entry was that it paid to be ready for the mean ones, those actively looking to keep people from entering the U.S. Those officials existed, and even if they only constituted an intimidating minority, they were the ones who cast an air of nervousness among recurring travelers.

As it turned out, racial profiling was a two-way street at the ports of entry.

"I hope I don't get the Filipino agent", you'd hear as the line slowly crept up to the booths, each individual advancing to whatever agent became available. Filipino agents had the reputation of being the toughest gatekeepers, the ones who would look into each person's document in excruciating detail, while white American officials were said to be the most relaxed and easy-going. The unofficial explanation behind the Filipino-American agents tougher and more rigorous demeanor was that they knew first-hand what it took to migrate to the U.S. legally, and they weren't about to let some Tijuanense cheat and abuse the system to work in the U.S. illegally –an occurrence that was all too common in all U.S. border towns and cities. Many Mexicans used to tourist visa to simply work in the U.S. unlawfully, returning home to Mexico at the end of each day. This is why tourist visas were particularly hard to obtain among those Mexican nationals who couldn't prove a steady source of substantial income in their country. Border officials knew how to sniff out those who claimed to visit for leisurely purposes but instead used their time in the U.S. to engage in remunerated activities. In their computer monitors, they could see the exact times at which an individual entered the U.S., as well as the exact times when they left. The data regarding travelers' departures from U.S. soil was made possible by the camera systems with facial and number plate recognition, which you could find on the American highways that reached the border with Mexico. The cameras were placed on the southbound lanes, after the last possible U.S. exit, effectively capturing any and all vehicles heading down to Mexico. In other words, the U.S. didn't even have to consult the records of Mexico's border authorities. Technology had made that unnecessary, which was just as well because Mexico is known to collaborate only halfheartedly on those matters, perhaps driven by a sense of duty not to snitch on its own people. Of course, this will never be Mexico's *official* excuse not to collaborate, but really, they don't need one; their much more modest resources at the border spoke for themselves.

The cameras were installed during Trump's administration, which really came down hard on any sort of border shenanigan that abused the good faith of U.S. border officials. If the entry and departure times of a frequent traveler hinted at a re-occurring pattern, indicating some sort of work schedule, border officials wouldn't take long to notice and, very probably, revoke the suspect's tourist visa altogether, essentially rendering any legal incursion across the border impossible. These punishments lasted as long as ten years, after which the perpetrator would have to issue an official apology addressed to the U.S. government, who would in turn decide whether to grant that person a second chance.

All of these repeated occurrences, mixed feelings of tediousness and worry, and tragicomic quirks were the everyday ingredients of life at the San Ysidro Port of Entry, the busiest border crossing on the planet. These unique idiosyncrasies had been the way roughly since September 11th, 2001.

And then came the pandemic.

*The children of different families mingled and played as if they'd
been friends for years, like neighbors without a neighborhood to
call their own.*

"They're good boys. Like all boys, they just want to play, and go to school, and draw, and play ball, and learn. We just want a place where they can do that and be left alone"

In spite of camping out in the street with no direct access to running water, everyone there seemed to put great efforts into keeping clean and dignified.

Jason, a native of Colón, Honduras, was feeling pretty good about his newly found job as an unloader at the Mercado Hidalgo.

José David and Wilson sported bright orange vests, given to them at the construction gig they landed the day before. For the rest of the group, they were an identifier of prosperity, a silver lining in a circumstance of sheer apprehension.

In Playas, it was not uncommon to find entire families of Amish and Mennonites from the Mid-West visiting Tijuana for its cheap and reliable medical services.

Bulnes, from San Pedro Sula, still carried a bullet buried in his thigh, courtesy of –you guessed it- gang members.

The border fence extended from hundreds of miles away, ran across the sandy beach and stretched out into the ocean, completing the split of North America in two.

His joke was met with laughter on the Mexican side only. Whether the Americans didn't understand Spanish, or simply were not in a laughing mood remained unclear.

On a clear day on Playas de Tijuana, it was possible to see the city of San Diego some twenty miles away, its skyline gleaming in the distance with splendorous dignity

Untethered by centuries of geopolitical differences, uninterrupted by the border patrol far below, the seagull chose to land gracefully on the beach of Tijuana.

Did you forget to buy a memento for your significant other? The sellers of la línea have your back.

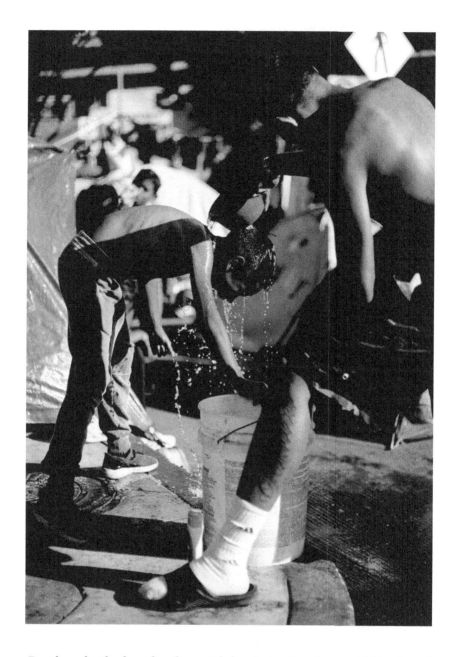

Brothers bathed each other with buckets of water and kids played hide-and-seek among the tents.

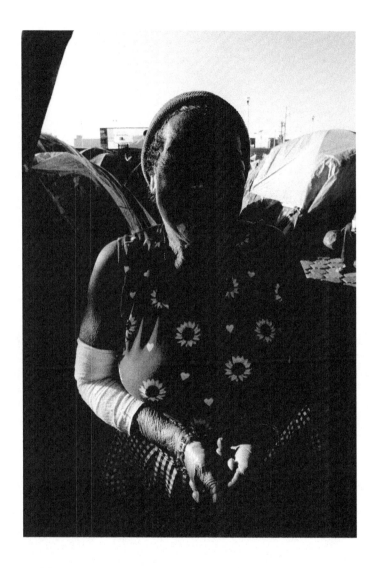

"I'm an old woman," Doña Natividad went on. "I have worked hard. I have been kind. I deserve a godly death. Una muerte de Dios." she said with aplomb. "It's when you die in peace, content, and you die because God calls you to his side, and not because some malandro shoots you in the street like a dog".

As I rested my head on the window and tried to get some sleep, we drove past an old sign riddled with bullet holes

As the volunteers came up with conjectures to explain the disappointing find, Octavio planted the white cross firmly in the ground.

"They look like repurposed detergent bottles or something," I said. "You'd think so, but no; it's an actual bottled water brand they sell in "Sonoyta",said Rubén. Indeed, as I crouched to inspect the abandoned bottle in detail, I read the eroded tag: Sun Water. The words were written in a fun, summery typography. It was yet another disturbing sign of the cynical but extremely lucrative businesses blossoming in this deathly industry.

3. The Shutdown.

One look at the border infrastructure is enough to let you know that they're ready to withstand and diligently deal with any sort of conflict caused by delinquent behavior. Drug trafficking, people smuggling, illegal trade, illicit employment... There's no doubt they could even come down a hypothetical breach and invasion of U.S. soil and resolve it without as much as breaking a sweat –as had indeed happened with the migrant caravan incident.

But there's one thing the border was most definitely not ready for: a viral pandemic.

In early March 2020, the world watched on the edge of their seats as the SARS-CoV-2 virus spread and seeped through every border on the planet. Much had been made of border fences and walls in the past years, beleaguered by all sorts of migrant and refugee crises. Now, those fences and walls proved to be futile in the defense of nations. The barbed wire, the impenetrable defense structures, the cutting-edge cameras, the police dogs, the movement sensors installed in the desert; they all proved to be useless in defending the nation from *the* foreign menace. The worst threat to mankind now didn't have an agenda, a flag, a religious creed, a political bias, or any ulterior motives to speak of. It was an invisible, minuscule particle, not complex enough to be a life form. But it was a deadly agent of chaos that rode on the coattails of mankind's indifference and self-assuredness, propagating a campaign of entropy and death.

The virus first appeared in China. Then it started spreading, notably to Iran, then Italy, then my beloved Spain... It had penetrated the Western world, the death tallies racking up with feverish impetus. Suddenly this wasn't one of those exotic diseases that only troubled Asian nations, like there had been so many in the past. The U.S. and Mexico knew it was a matter of time before the insidious calamity reached homeland.

For a few weeks, the virus hit California hard while it seemed everything was smooth sailing in Tijuana. American hospitals quickly became saturated with patients and depleted of medical supplies, while the virus' deathly scythe appeared to neglect Mexico altogether. For the first time in the history of Tijuana, it felt like it was probably a good thing that so many Americans didn't even consider Tijuana as a place worth visiting. But that didn't take away from the fact that thousands of *tijuanenses* crossed the border daily, carrying out their lives with one foot in Mexico and the other in the U.S. And yet, the days went by, and all seemed normal.

At this time, the virus was the protagonist of all sorts of wild theories and hopeful ruminations. Maybe, just maybe, Mexico would be off the hook for some reason. The Mexican president, Andrés Manuel López Obrador, even floated the idea that Mexicans would withstand the virus on account of having strong genes. And if that wasn't reassuring enough, he appeared on national TV showing off his indigenous amulets which he swore would give him all the protection he needed. He even urged the Mexican people to keep hugging and kissing and not give in to the fears brewing outside the country's borders. And for a brief few days, he might as well have been correct. Mexico, a country with over fifty million people living in poverty, a country where healthcare is mediocre at best, a country whose capital is one of the most densely populated cities in the world... Mexico seemed to be doing just fine, while the U.S. and Europe endured what seemed like a modern viral apocalypse.

It was a time of eerie calm on the south side of the border, a few days in which it seemed that nobody wanted to be the first to throw up their hands in panic and declare an official emergency. During those days, however, small signs of impending doom began to appear. There was a notable scarcity of canned foods at the supermarket. People started to keep a considerable distance from one another. Some casually wrapped scarves around their mouths, even when the weather didn't warrant such accessories. And then there was the issue of the border. Everyone *knew* it was only a matter of time before they shut it down indefinitely, effectively truncating the fruitful symbiosis between San Diego and Tijuana. The question was *when* exactly that would happen. There was even some debate regarding who would be the first to shut its doors to its neighbor; Mexico, or the U.S. For once, Mexico seemed to have a perfectly valid reason to unilaterally keep out American travelers, but it was doubtful that such a move would come to pass. At least, not until the U.S. did the same to them first. One way or the other, the highly dynamic border of Tijuana was about to experience a drastic cessation in crossings. This much was common knowledge, so much so that the lines to cross to California became exponentially longer in the days preceding the shutdown. Imprudent as they were, Mexican nationals wanted to make the most of Tijuana's beautiful half-sister, San Diego.

For my wife and I this time was particularly unnerving because she was due to give birth to our second child in little more than a month. We had planned for the birth to be on American soil; all the arrangements –and corresponding payments- had been made. It bears mentioning that, although there is no official policy against it, it is commonly frowned upon when a foreigner enters the U.S. with the sole purpose of giving birth to an American baby. Mexicans who can afford such a privilege do it all the time. Yes, the birth is significantly more expensive than what it would cost in Mexico, but the resulting blue passport makes it a worthwhile investment for the child, especially when hailing from a country marked by instability such as Mexico, and –it pains me to say it- Spain. This is, however, a first step in the much-criticized chain migration phenomenon; at the age of twenty-one, that American baby born to foreign parents will be able to sponsor them for U.S. residence. The parents will in turn do the same to their parents, siblings, cousins... And before you know it, that baby turns out to be the first link in a lengthy chain of bureaucratically manufactured Americans. Many on the right have vehemently suggested that the 14th amendment needs... well, amending. Written in 1866, it states that: *"All persons born or naturalized in the United States, and subject to the jurisdiction thereof, are citizens of the United States and the State wherein they reside."* It was originally intended to incorporate the descendants of African slaves into the fabric of the young nation. In other words, the 14th amendment was meant to right the wrong of bringing people to U.S. soil against their will to exploit them in inhumane ways; it was passed the year after slavery was abolished. The angry claim is that, in the 21st century, the 14th amendment constitutes a loophole, as it was envisioned to address a problem that no longer exists. Besides, it is now significantly more feasible to travel to the U.S. from any corner of the world than it was when it was written, so it's a loophole prone to be exploited at an ever-increasing scale. Loophole or not, my wife and I were going to make the most of it –as we had done with our first daughter.

The border crossing is particularly awkward for a pregnant woman who is not an American national. My wife always asked me is she should wear clothes that minimize the prominence of the baby bump.

"No", I told her. "What you're doing is perfectly legal. Just show your hospital appointment and your receipts."

"What if they ask me why I'm having the baby in the U.S.?"

This question indeed was a common occurrence. Many mothers-to-be resolved in making up some phony claim that their baby presented a health issue that would be better taken care of in the U.S. They even had to provide a doctor's note to prove it (doctors in Tijuana were perfectly accustomed to fabricating these types of notes full of half-truths and whole lies in order to help out expecting mothers). The way I saw it, there was something sinister about making up fraudulent claims about your unborn baby's health.

"We just tell them the truth", I told my wife. "We simply want to have the baby in San Diego. And it's perfectly legal too".

Despite the legality of the act, border officials could torment you with questions between the lines of which you could perfectly sense their ideological bias. *"Can't you have your baby in Mexico? Are there no hospitals in Mexico? Last I checked, Mexicans were born in Mexico".* One simply had to endure the interrogation knowing that, in the end, you'd be let through. After all, no border official in their right mind wants to put a pregnant woman through an overly stressful situation. The risk is too high for all involved.

We held out in Tijuana as long as we thought we could afford to while the rumors of the border shutdown intensified. The paranoia in the city grew and grew, even if there had only been a couple of confirmed Covid-19 cases. Of course, that was only *confirmed* cases. People knew not to trust any figure published by the Mexican government, which up to this point had been stubbornly trying to play down the gravity of the impending health crisis. And then there was the high transmission rate, the long incubation period, and all the other particularities of a deadly virus that, at that point, was almost untraceable. When it came to tallying Covid cases, authorities were chasing shadows. Meanwhile people carried on with their way of life; weddings, communions, *carne asadas, quinceañeras, quermeses, taquizas*, galas, church events... These types of get-togethers were cornerstones in the essentially joyous and community-oriented Mexican culture. But at that time, the one having the real party was an uninvited guest in all of them; the SARS-CoV-2 virus.

The pandemic was among us. It was not yet official, and no government measures had been put into effect yet. But its presence could be *felt*. Rumors that hospitals were filling up fast reached everyone's ears. People began to self-quarantine. The park outside our home, always filled with the cheers and yelling of children, was now shrouded in an uncanny, quiet stillness. Neighbors that knew of my wife's advanced pregnancy began to message us; *"They're going to shut the border any second now. What are you doing still here?"* We agreed. It was time to go.

In haste, we found a rental apartment in San Diego and swiftly packed our things. My wife's 35-week baby bump was anything but imperceptible. At the border booth, the agent took our passports. His eyes went directly to my wife's perfectly rounded belly.

"Where are you off to today?"

"We're going to San Diego before they shut down the border. We're going to have our baby there", my wife replied nonchalantly.

The official stared at us in silence. He turned to his computer monitor and started typing. I tried to hide my nervousness. I knew what we were doing was legal, but this was the turf of The Man. I always got nervous here. It was inevitable for me. My wife, however, seemed cool as a cucumber. Had she been a little too forthcoming? Had she come across as cheeky? The agent proceeded with the proverbial border official poker face.

"Anything to declare?" the agent asked.

"No. Well, just the unborn baby." my wife responded with a smile.

I think I froze a little bit. *'No jokes at the border'*, I thought to myself. And as far as the joke went, had it even landed well? Or had it evocated the grim picture of an unborn baby inside our vehicle's trunk? My wife caressed her belly with a tender smile, as if to drive home the remark.

The agent looked at her, his lips curling into... a smile? He handed us our passports back.

"All right, ma'am", he said. "Good luck and congratulations."

"Thank you, sir", we responded in unison.

We were through.

The following day, the crossing from the U.S. to Mexico was shut down indefinitely. Only the very few who could provide proof of essential traveling were allowed through. People didn't know it then, but the restrictions would last for well over a year.

4. A tale of two countries.

Our second daughter was born into a world in quarantine. We ended up staying in San Diego for three months. As the first wave of the pandemic was slowing down in the advent of the summer, we moved back to Tijuana. It was particularly curious to see how people in the U.S. and Mexico had taken to life in a pandemic. My overall impression was that both countries were dealing with it equally well, or equally badly –depending on how benevolent or cynical you wanted to be about at it. This pandemic had caught the entire world off-guard, and the information about the virus was still dubious and at times even contradictory. Each country dealt with the pandemic in vastly different ways, revealing a great deal about their respective national mindsets. Besides, the obstacles each region faced under the pandemic were very different. Mexico's problems included, (but were not limited to) the insufficient healthcare infrastructure, the abundant misinformation about the virus (at times even proposed by Mexico's central government), and the fact that most Mexicans couldn't simply go home and carry on working from their computers. The country relied heavily on hands-on industries in the primary and secondary sectors, as well as on the visit of millions of tourists from abroad. All of these activities would be deemed non-essential during the worst moments of the pandemic; the Mexican economy, it seemed, was on the verge of total collapse. And yet, for a country that is used to having a lackluster economy, insufficient infrastructure, and around forty percent of its inhabitants living in moderate to extreme poverty, there was a sense that the pandemic couldn't possibly bring that much more additional havoc. It was like sounding off an alarm in a place where alarms had been blaring for over two hundred years, after which they'd simply become an everyday background drone. As the viral incidence started to soar, an unsettling sense of normalcy prevailed on the streets; for millions of Mexicans, weathering out the storm from the comforts of their homes simply was not an option.

"I have to go out to make a living", they'd say. "It's a simple choice, really; I must choose between maybe dying from this virus or certainly dying of starvation. I will take my chances with the virus".

This was the line of thought professed by millions of Mexicans whose every day revolved around the struggle against their immediate circumstance. All that they asked of the world was that they'd have something to put on their dinner plate come sundown. Can a state that has so failed its people ask them now to stay home and take one for the team? For the millions of disenfranchised Mexicans, the pandemic didn't change anything; it was, as it always had been, every man for himself. I cringed whenever I heard that Mexico's greatest hindrance during the pandemic was its people's ignorance. Educated or not, the mechanics of the virus were not so hard to grasp. My two-year-old toddler soon understood all the new do's and don'ts and abided religiously. That's not to say that people were not negligent or careless in the way they wore their masks (or didn't wear them) or the way they still gathered in large numbers –this being a prevalent phenomenon among the more affluent people who could afford to throw a proverbially massive Mexican fiesta. But as far as the millions of people trying to survive in densely populated cities, ignorance wasn't the issue. Rather, a complete lockup in urban Mexico was utopia. Far too many people relied on the informal economies of peddling, chauffeuring, street performing, and other such activities. After a couple of weeks, when the virus had dug its claws firmly into the country, these quintessential characters of the urban Mexican landscape carried on with their business as usual, only now they did it with masks on.

⌒⌒⌒

The virus in the U.S. was a completely different story. Whereas Mexico simply didn't have the medical infrastructure to accommodate the soaring number of Covid-19 patients, the U.S. was home to the most advanced medical facilities... and a population that couldn't afford them. Thus, the country that had made snake oil salesmen rich in the past now saw a brand new wave of impostors advertising baloney home remedies against Covid-19. These ranged from blow-drying hot air into your own throat to drinking bleach. Televangelists with viewership in the millions would also push their expensive false medicines made of silver solutions. Other less business savvy preachers would urge their faithful to forego any sort of medical precaution and trust that God would protect them.

And then there were the millions of people who believed that being made to wear a mask was an affront to their freedom. The United States' obsessive preoccupation with freedom was, in fact, catalyzing the shackling of the nation under the death-dealing clasp of the virus. When freedom is valued higher than life itself, it becomes something of an absurd folly. Of course, to entertain this thought is to concede that antiviral masks did indeed curtail an individual's freedom. But how exactly? I tried long and hard to grasp this point of view, which, in my understanding, must have had a solid origin in order to be so widely extended and accepted. As a foreigner, the mere idea that masks could make me any less free seemed preposterous; perhaps, I told myself, I was missing some information, a nuance about the American way of life that was going over my head. No other country on earth had been home to such spirited backlash against mask mandates. And yet, in the U.S. it had somehow become a political problem. I thought, perhaps, that if the American left, -who proclaimed to be the only true partisans of science in the political spectrum- accepted masks as a necessary step to fight the virus, the American right should reject the face coverings if only out of oppositional duty. I wondered if the so-called 'anti-maskers' were acting out their true beliefs, as attained and refined after much critical deliberation, or if they were simply being carried along with the contrarian mob. Their arguments, if fallacious, were pretty straightforward. There was the sense that any collective effort in pursuit of a communal good amounted to socialism. Even if it came down to as simple a gesture as wearing a mask in public, the state couldn't tell people what to do, lest it be a totalitarian state. Suddenly, the cultural pillars that were rugged individualism and the proverbial American liberty had become misconstrued to the point of being an impediment to the country's overall wellbeing. President Trump himself challenged the necessity of mask wearing, and, if one were to judge from the news, it seemed like rejecting the little mouthpieces had become the newest cornerstone in the American right's collective identity.

However, the political spectrum had become particularly polarized in the past few years, and I had to remind myself that what I saw on the news and on social media shone light on those two very loud and defiant polar extremes, and that the vast majority of the American people, be they left or right leaning, probably didn't think to make a political issue out of the masks. This thought gave me some peace. In all my years dealing with American people, I had found them to be kind, considerate and decent. The confinement that resulted from the pandemic had truncated everyday interactions with normal folks, and the only glimpse we got into the world outside was through biased and cherry-picked news and social media stories. I had to remind myself that those scandalous stories were fringe cases not indicative of the world at large.

Being a foreigner also gave me some helpful perspective, as I had watched closely how the pandemic unfolded in Spain, Mexico, and in the U.S. Both Spain and Mexico had leftist governments, whereas the U.S. was under a right wing presidency. The virus had caught all three countries with their pants down, and all three governments had wasted precious time downplaying the severity of the pandemic, even after the writing had been on the wall for weeks. It wasn't a matter of left or right; it was a matter of human complacence.

Strangely, as families locked themselves up at home, as each nation shut itself off from the rest of the world, it seemed that the human race was becoming more united than ever. For once, everybody had one common enemy. It was a time when you could no longer hug your friends, but during which people were constantly keeping up with the international news and each country's efforts against the virus. The individual became isolated, while the collective became united. The world came together around one event, but unlike the World Cup, now everybody rooted for everybody; if there was to be one winner, it'd would be the folks who first came up with a vaccine.

As everyday life came to a standstill, a new sense of appreciation arose around those individuals who kept the world functioning minimally. In the U.S. the jobs deemed essential to keep the world spinning were often carried out by immigrants; farmers, laborers, factory workers, nurses, loaders, truck drivers... For a few months, much of the migrant community at the lower rungs of the economy proved to be more important than CEOs and celebrities. The pandemic turned out to be the great equalizer, leveling all sorts of nations to similar states of hardship. People everywhere lost their jobs, their health, and their lives. I wondered if the worldwide crisis would have some bearing on the migrant flows of the world, now that the pandemic had revealed that, beneath the varying flags and different degrees of affluence, people were largely the same, had the same vulnerabilities, and yearned for the same simple things such as friends and family, health and a sense of purpose. But as the months went by and the world became more adept at dealing with the virus, there was a growing sense that the crisis would pass and things would go back to the way they were, to the old hierarchy, to a world of prosperous nations and beggarly ones. The global pandemic would then be a distant bleep in the radar of the collective memory, and downtrodden individuals would once again seek to make an exodus to more promising lands.

5. Remain in Mexico.

In the last two years of Trump's presidency, the *Remain in Mexico* program was put into effect as a binational effort with the neighboring country to the south. This program proposed that all migrants who arrived at the border looking to attain political asylum would not be allowed into the U.S. until their cases had been resolved favorably. In the meantime, they would be allowed to wait in Mexico. This program was conceived after the Trump administration's 'zero tolerance' stance led to ghastly situations such as migrant families being separated and children being put in cages at border detention centers. The Trump administration alleged that such measures had been put in place by the previous president, Barack Obama, and that they were necessary to ascertain if the people claiming to be families were in fact related, as many human traffickers carried other people's children into the U.S. while posing as their parents. The remedy was deemed to be worse than the problem when cases of detained migrant children dying made the headlines and the detention centers' inhumane conditions elicited comparisons to concentration camps. Thus, the Trump administration resolved in simply refusing to house asylum seekers on U.S. soil. They delegated the bulk of the problem to Mexico, and that is how the *Remain in Mexico* program was born.

Contrary to what may seem logical, Mexican president Andrés Manuel Lopez Obrador, (who leaned very far left but had found common ground with Trump as a fellow populist,) was keen to collaborate on this program; while Trump reckoned he was turning the Mexican border cities into a waiting room for his proverbial *'bad hombres'*, AMLO saw it as an opportunity to utilize the migrant masses as workforce in the very industrial cities of Northern Mexico, while also giving this region a makeover in public perception. After all, border cities like Tijuana (Baja California), Juárez (Chihuahua) and Reynosa and Matamoros (Tamaulipas) had international renown as some of the most violent cities on the planet. Perhaps, the Mexican president hoped, this welcoming attitude toward the migrant community would afford these regions better reputations.

Activists on both sides of the border lambasted the *Remain in Mexico* program. In fact, *'Remain in Mexico'* was an informal name, as the program's official title was *'Migrant Protection Protocols'*, a choice of words regarded to be either very unfortunate or willfully tongue-in-cheek. After all, what protection does the program offer if it causes thousands of migrants to camp out in the streets of such crime-infested cities? The migrants, who had endured a diaspora of biblical proportions, fleeing precisely from organized crime, now found themselves without a roof, turned into sitting ducks for delinquents of all sorts. AMLO may have harbored philanthropic and blissful hopes for the MPP program, but reality quickly showed that regional and federal authorities had insufficient bandwidth to start to make it work. Many locals grew resentful of the refugees as they gathered in growing numbers and started to cause disruption and unrest in the streets. Xenophobic messages and opinions started making the rounds, even though the migrant community was largely composed of Mexicans from other parts of the country.

Despite all this, as Mexico dealt with the knots and bolts of an impossible project, the impression in Washington D.C. was that the Migrants Protection Protocols program actually *worked*. After all, the real intention behind this program was to deter people from migrating to the U.S., and as such, the program had shown some success. Indeed, many migrants ended up assimilating to life in Mexico and chose to make that their final destination instead of perpetuating an uncertain and distressing waiting game. Others found themselves having to choose between living in a foreign city that was dangerous, and their hometowns filled with similar perils, and gave new meaning to the phrase *"the house always wins"*; if your destiny is to die a violent death, you might as well arrange for it to happen closer to home.

The pandemic worsened the situation of the *Remain in Mexico* migrants significantly. Many of them lost their jobs when the country decreed a mandatory standstill. Attention to the migrants fell by the wayside as the whole country tended to the new global menace. The Immigration offices in Mexico closed their doors indefinitely, thus extending the migratory legal limbo many migrants were in. In a world where every nation began to close its doors and barricade its borders, it was a terrible time to be stateless.

Following a particularly convulsive election, a changing of the guard was fast approaching in the United States. For the first time in almost thirty years, a president who ran for a second period would be voted out of office. Trump was due to exit the White House on January 20th, 2021 and it was presumed that the outspokenly hostile rhetoric against undocumented migrants would leave the oval office along with him. Joe Biden would occupy the presidency after running a campaign based on the healing of the nation (as the country had seen unprecedented polarization among the American people during the Trump years). In regard to his attitude toward the illegal immigration phenomenon, Biden assured during his campaign that he would end the Remain in Mexico program "on day one", promising that any and all migrants hoping to attain political asylum on American soil would be allowed into the country while their cases were being reviewed. But after landing the presidency, Biden began to show a more restrained and cautious demeanor when discussing the migrant crisis, and admitted that he couldn't simply cancel the Remain in Mexico program overnight. Nonetheless, he carried on promising humane solutions to the border crisis, but always did so in very vague terms.

"Nothing has changed", said Graciela Parra with a slight eye roll. "MPP is still very much in place, but now that Trump is out of the picture, the migrants feel they have better chances", she explained.

Graciela was the operations coordinator at the Scalabrini center in Tijuana, a place more commonly known as La Casa del Migrante (The Migrant Home). It was located in the neighborhood of Buena Vista, (*good views*). This barrio was aptly named for having a scenic vantage point over Tijuana, as it stood on the edge of a steep hill overlooking the city. The neighborhood itself, however, was impoverished and dilapidated, with many houses barely hanging on to the dusty cliff. Nonetheless, La Casa del Migrante stood with grandeur like the honorable institution that it was, at once modest in its structural appearance and highly respected and admired by the community. Above its entrance was a text in bulky metallic letters:

"Yo andaba de extranjero, y tú me acogiste".

This was a verse from the Bible, specifically from Matthew 25:35; *"I was a foreigner, and you welcomed me in."* The center had been founded by the missionaries of Saint Charles Borromeo, also known as the Scalabrinian missionaries, who in turn were the ideation of one Giovanni Battista Scalabrini, an Italian priest who achieved great renown as a defender of migrants, refugees and displaced persons in the second half of the 19th century. Scalabrini had accompanied waves of destitute Italian migrants as they sought better futures in Brasil and the U.S. at the turn of the century. His charismatic demeanor and successful pursuits led the popes of the time to believe that Scalabrini would be a worthy addition to the cardinalate. However, they were unable to convince him to accept a high rank in Rome, as Scalabrini was certain that his true vocation was helping the downtrodden migrant community across the globe. Keeping the order's charismas intact, Scalabrini soon began to reach out to migrant peoples of other nationalities and to establish shelters all over the world. More than a century after Father Giovanni's death, the Scalabrinian migrant center in Tijuana is one of his order's most robust bastions.

Graciela was in her early thirties, although her focused resolve and serious demeanor granted her a certain air of wisdom beyond her years. She walked me through the lobby corridor and onto a large indoor patio around which the building rose up four stories. The staircases and the doors to each room all were visible from the courtyard, giving the whole structure an air of openness and familiarity. It reminded me of the building from *El Chavo del*

Ocho, an old Mexican television show about a tightly knit community of neighbors. It was close to lunchtime and a delicious smell emanated from the kitchen by the patio.

"Who does the cooking?" I asked Graciela.

"We have a chef. She works with our volunteers and with the migrants. We all do our part here", she explained.

We walked past a room in which a few children were dancing to a flashy and colorful disco-themed videogame projected on the wall. Graciela peeked in.

"And you didn't invite me? Buuuuh!" she said with a laugh. She turned to me and added: "We have to keep the children active. It's been hard, you know, with the pandemic…"

We arrived at a large empty room with computers.

"Are those donations?" she asked me, pointing at the bags I was carrying.

"Yes. I brought mostly men's clothes. All in good shape, just a bit worn out." I responded.

"Thank you. You can leave them over there by the wall."

"I also brought diapers. My girl outgrew these before she could use them."

"Mmh… We don't have babies here at the moment, but you can leave them with us, and I'll be sure to pass them on to the right place" Graciela said.

She explained that La Casa del Migrante was intended only for single men or men with families. There were other specific migrant shelters for women who travelled alone and women who travelled with children. Being one of the biggest and longest-standing migrant shelters in Tijuana, La Casa del Migrante was like a leader to the rest of the shelters. Oftentimes, donations would arrive here in bulk and Graciela would orchestrate their distribution to more fitting locations.

Graciela opened the windows to let the air in.

"I know it's cold, but we're very cautious of outside visitors. This pandemic has made me a big believer in ventilation", she said.

"Oh, of course. I have come to share the same philosophy", I told her.

"What a year it's been...! But hey; we're still here," she said with pride.

Graciela went on to narrate how the migrant shelter had had to close its doors to new migrants for the first three months of the pandemic.

"It was tough" she said. "Everything stopped with the pandemic; everything except migratory flows."

To make matters worse, migrants who had lived in the shelter in the past but managed to move out to places of their own had begun dropping by once more hoping to get a room.

"Many migrants that had started to get ahead in Tijuana lost their jobs in the pandemic. They suddenly found themselves unable to pay rent and came back here hoping to stay with us once more. But we had to turn them away. This shelter is strictly for folks who have just arrived in Tijuana."

Even though they had to reject these unfortunate profiles, La Casa del Migrante always went out of its way to help them land new jobs; the shelter had close connections to over one hundred employers in Tijuana. In fact, over the years, the shelter had become much more than just a place to keep migrants from sleeping in the street. Here, they could find the help of legal counselors, psychologists, social workers and family therapists.

The schools of Tijuana had not yet reopened, so the shelter had become an improvised daycare facility for young children. Older kids also dropped by on a daily basis to use the shelter's computers to attend their online classes. Their joyful yelling and stampeding runs echoed across the building.

"Now we have around twenty children who are with us practically every day from 7am to 7pm. They need a place to stay while their parents are out working."

Graciela spoke of how the migrant shelter went to great lengths to break harmful patterns routinely repeated in humble Latin American households.

"It's a very cultural thing; children are made to stay home and look after the younger siblings. We provide the support to break that pattern and make the parents understand that such arrangements are a problem. Children need to be children. They need to have fun and receive an education, not devote their time to things the adults should be doing."

She also explained the shelter's zero tolerance approach to machismo, another insidious constant across many Latin American households.

"For instance, we have a rule here whereby it's the men who wash the dishes. At first, this simple rule is very shocking to some men, and even some women, who will still have sexist behaviors ingrained in them as a normal thing."

"Have there been incidents with the migrants? Any... uncomfortable situations?"

Graciela sighed.

"Oh, yes… Many of them have a lot of baggage," she explained. "They have been through a lot and seen all sorts of horrible things. So a few resort to substance abuse…"

"How do you deal with that?"

"Every case is different. But we offer help to rehabilitate them. However, many have persisted in their vice and… We have had to kick out some migrants in the past, yes…"

From the window, we saw a family of six migrants get into a bus with the government logo. The youngest kid must have been around eight.

"Where are they off to?" I asked.

"*El hotel filtro*" responded Graciela. *The Filter Hotel.*

"Is that an actual hotel?" I asked.

"No", said Graciela. "It's a government facility, but I can't tell you where it is. I mean, I don't know myself where it is; the location is undisclosed. It's just a place the migrants go to be observed and cared for while they do quarantine."

"Why do they call it *hotel filtro*?" I inquired, and Graciela once again rolled her eyes with not-so-subtle resignation.

"I know, it's a terrible name…" she lamented. "I don't know why everyone started calling it that. It doesn't help us. When the migrants hear '*hotel*', they say: '*But I can't afford a hotel.*' When they hear '*filter*', they say: '*Does that mean some of us won't be accepted at the shelter?*' It's… a poor choice of words, for sure."

The inadequately named 'filter hotel' was a necessary step to keep any possible Covid-19 outbreaks from ravaging through the shelter.

"We do all we can to keep safe, but there's only so much you can do", Graciela explained. "For instance, every day many migrants go out to the city to work from sunup to sundown. There's no way of knowing if they take precautions like we ask them to. But I'd like to think they do, because the fact is we've had no outbreaks here."

Graciela spoke proudly of how the shelter found migrants work and a sense of immediate purpose while they waited for the U.S. to decide their fate. The paperwork was tediously slow, and had become even more sluggish with the pandemic. Having a day-to-day routine to be able to focus on smaller-scale aspects of life proved to be of great psychological help for the migrants. And while some of them found contentment in Tijuana to the point that they decided to stay there for good, most would leave for the border in a hurry once the U.S. authorities summoned them.

"So many families are leaving from one day to the next. They leave personal possessions here, uncashed checks, friendships and acquaintances that never find out what became of them..." Graciela said throwing up her hands in disbelief. "Many times, the Tijuana employers call us because the migrants simply stop showing up, and it's down to us to explain that the migrants have been finally called to the U.S. It's a bit of a bureaucratic pain, but most employers simply ask us to send in another candidate for an interview. We work with people who understand this... unusual dynamic." Graciela said with a smile.

I asked Graciela if President Biden was really being more gracious to the migrants than his predecessor. She shook her head with a weary smile, and explained that, while the change in tone was appreciated, the same old policies prevailed pretty much untouched, as the characteristics a migrant had to fulfill to be deemed a political refugee remained exactly the same.

"But migrants flock to the border now because they really think Biden has an open borders policy. It simply isn't true", she said categorically.

What Biden *had* begun to do was to slowly roll back the Remain in Mexico program. Thus, asylum seekers would be beckoned into the U.S. only to end up occupying the very same detention facilities Trump was so harshly criticized for. The news regarding these events were murky, opaque, filled with euphemisms from the left looking to cut Biden some slack and opportunist and callous whataboutism from the right.

As far as the migrants were concerned, what mattered most is that they were finally being allowed into U.S. territory. Graciela described how hundreds of migrants had started to camp out in San Ysidro merely a couple of days after Biden was declared the new president. She suspected there was sometimes a certain level of deceit involved in their strategy.

"It doesn't take a couple days to travel from Central America to Tijuana. So I think these are migrants who have been here in Tijuana for quite some time, who have maybe experienced a bad turn of luck with the pandemic, and are now liking their chances with the new president", she explained. "They camp out as if they had just arrived from their home countries, to give their presence an air of urgency. After all, once you have acquired a legal resident status in Mexico, once you've found a job, and a relatively stable and safe environment, it becomes harder to prove you desperately *need* political asylum."

Graciela's suspicions seemed well grounded. But, as I had done a couple of years before with the migrant caravan, I felt the urge to visit the protagonists in the streets and hear their testimonies from their own point of view.

6. Muerte de Dios.

The testimonies I heard at the entrance of the San Ysidro port of entry were sadly all too similar to the ones I heard a couple of years before when the caravans arrived. Migrants were still running away from abject poverty and gang-related violence -the tragic constants in so many Latin American hot zones. There was, however, one significant addition to the calamitous catalogue of reasons to leave one's land; two hurricanes had hit Honduras in the span of three weeks in November 2020, ravaging through the country and causing floods that further brought the country to its knees after a year of violence, political unrest, and a pandemic. The very name of Honduras, which literally means *'depths'*, seemed now more than ever an omen of the country's perennial sinking into new abysses of misfortune and hardship.

I did notice some things had changed in comparison to my previous visits to the refugee campsites. Whereas the caravans had merely occupied the plaza that is found directly in front of the port of entry, this new encampment was much more disorganized and sprawled into the surrounding streets. There seemed to be more migrants, but this time around there were far fewer volunteers and reporters. I figured that the ports of entry that were garnering most of the media attention were the ones in Texas, as that state was home to many of the controversial migrant detention centers the news were focusing on. In Tijuana, however, the migrants seemed to have been left to their devices, bereft of any solid guidance from migration experts or any guarantee from U.S.

authorities. Perhaps more concerning was the fact that around half of the migrants in the tightly packed campsite lived as if there was no Covid-19 to speak of, foregoing any of the precautions that the world had learned by heart at this point after a whole year of pandemic.

"Aren't you folks concerned about Covid-19?" I asked a man by the name of José Rodríguez, from Olancho (Honduras).

"Mmmh... Every morning the Red Cross shows up and checks all of our temperatures," he explained. "Other than that, I can't say we take it too seriously, to be perfectly honest."

José had been camping out on the streets with his wife and daughter for over a month, but he had already been living in Mexico for over two years. In other words, he seemed to validate Graciela's concerns. In fact, José himself claimed that he would like to appear *freshly arrived at the border*, as it were, but also admitted that was not an option anymore.

"My daughter Ximena was born here; she's Mexican. There's no use in us saying we just arrived here from Honduras, as our little baby would give us away with her Mexican papers", José laughed.

"But, José, that shouldn't change anything", José's wife pointed out. "The fact is that, while we were here, the hurricane destroyed our home in Honduras and now the *maras* are building on our property..."

"Oh, yes..." José said somberly. "The reason we left Honduras in the first place is very much still there."

"The gangs?" I asked.

"Correct", he responded, and his wife nodded gravely. The eight-month-old baby in her arms kicked about and smiled at the lively ambience around her.

"Why did you decide to camp out here?" I asked.

"President Biden made a promise. He said he would help migrants get their papers. We're still waiting for specific details, but hey; he already made the promise", José responded.

Part of me wanted to tell José that maybe he had been misguided; that perhaps he was ill informed about what Biden would proceed to do. Heck, part of me wanted to grab José by the collar and shake him while vehemently reminding him that he should never take a politician's promise to the bank, and that it was not responsible to camp out in the streets for many cold weeks with a baby barely a few months old. Then, another part of me considered that I couldn't possibly imagine what José had been through, and that perhaps staying in his home would have been the most irresponsible thing of all.

"How is Ximena? Doing well?" I asked.

"She's healthy and happy, *gracias a Dios*", the parents responded.

The baby did look plump and joyful, and if it wasn't obvious from her age, her adorable smile let everyone know she was perfectly oblivious to the havoc surrounding her.

"I'm glad to hear it", I said.

I looked around me and noticed that this time there seemed to be more children at the camp. Brothers bathed each other with buckets of water; kids played hide-and-seek among the many tents; and girls played and pranced around the campsite as local police reminded them to keep to the sidewalks. I perused the camp with the camera hanging from my neck, hoping to get testimonies from migrants of all stripes. They were much more diverse than the mostly Central American caravans of the past; besides the many Hondurans, Salvadorans, and Guatemalans, I also met Venezuelans, Cubans, Ecuadorians, and Haitians, as well as large numbers from central and southern Mexico. Most migrants were happy to speak to me, but some rejected having their photograph taken.

"No, no photos, please", said Fernando, a man in his fifties from Guerrero after I asked him if I could take his portrait as he shaved over a bucket of water. We had been talking for a while, and I found the image of him carefully grooming his facial hair amidst such chaos to be particularly poetic. "If you take a photo and somehow it gets around, they could find out we're here", he said as he rubbed shaving soap to his cheeks and looked in a tiny mirror intently.

"Who's they?" I asked.

He looked up from the mirror.

"Why, the narcos, of course," he responded gravely.

Fernando's wife, Cristina, nodded in agreement smiling timidly.

"Yes, it's true", she lamented. "We're sorry".

"I know you looked for the most handsome man in the camp and found me," joked Fernando. "So I understand your frustration!"

"Oh, don't be sorry!" I laughed. "I'll find someone -not half as good looking, but they'll have to do."

The three of us laughed together. It felt good to share a moment of levity with them. It felt even better that it had been Fernando who got the joke going. I imagine good humor is an indispensable ally when embarking on a trip as treacherous and uncertain as the one they were on, a trip catalyzed overnight by violence and fear.

"The narcos wanted to buy our land and our house. I refused, because why would I give up what I have worked for all of my life?" he said looking in my eyes.

"But they wouldn't take no for an answer. They killed our nephew and made threats against the entire family", Cristina recalled.

"So, in the middle of the night, we just upped and left. But before we parted…" Fernando's eyes welled up. "I set my house on fire. I wasn't about to let those bastards get the fruit of all my life's work. I preferred to burn the whole thing to the ground."

Cristina caressed his man's back as he relived the painful episode.

"Anyway, we're not out of the woods yet" she said. "We are trying to be as discreet as possible." She lowered her voice as her eyes darted to the policemen supervising the campsite from the street. "We think the narcos are in touch with the Tijuana police, so we'd rather keep a low profile so nobody knows our whereabouts."

Fernando looked at me.

"We're not paranoid" he assured me. "A lot of us in this camp are in similar predicaments. Some of them have received mysterious calls saying: *'I know you're in Tijuana'* and things like that. That is why we have destroyed our cellphones. We don't want to be tracked in any way…"

After hearing Fernando's story, I decided I'd put the lens cap on my camera as I perused the migrant campsite. It was a small gesture, but one that I hoped would convey to the migrants that I wasn't there to simply photograph them without their consent and unknowingly expose them to danger. I did find many migrants, particularly on the younger side, became interested in my presence there and approached me to strike up conversation upon recognizing my Spanish accent. As always, the topic of discussion tended to be European soccer. A young man from Salvador named Marlon wore an Atlético de Madrid jersey, which we proudly displayed to me.

"Look, it's the official jersey from their last UEFA Europe League win", he said with pride.

"My man, I'm a Real Madrid fan," I told him in a jokingly haughty tone. Marlon laughed.

"I'll be the one bragging this season. The league is ours!" he said.

"Enjoy it, as it could be the only one in the next twenty years!" I quipped.

"But, you see, *that's* why Atlético is my team", Marlon said with inspiration as he tapped the team's emblem on the jersey. "*That's* why this jersey gives me strength during all of this."

"What do you mean?" I asked.

"It's easy to be a Real Madrid fan. You guys are used to winning," he explained. "But Atlético? We're not about winning. We're about enduring. We're about pushing forward. We're about taking the blows and not losing hope. As a migrant, there's a lot of useful stuff in Atlético's philosophy."

I had never considered how something as supposedly trivial as a sport could give migrants the spiritual nourishment Marlon was describing. He spoke from the heart and claimed that life is not so much about racking one victory on top of another, but rather about moving from failure to failure without losing hope.

"That is the only way to live; coming to terms with the fact that some things are simply out of our control…" he said pensively.

"What do you think will happen when you finally cross to the U.S.? Will you be welcomed in or turned away?" I asked him bluntly.

"I sincerely do not know. All I know if that I have endured a lot to get here. From this point on… it's out of my control", he concluded.

As I advanced parallel to the tight formation of tents, an old woman pointed to my camera and yelled:

"Well, if you're going to be taking photos, give us some money in exchange!"

"Of course, ma'am," I said. "What's your name?"

"Doña Natividad Peña, from Yoro, Honduras" she said graciously. She was a short woman with weathered hands and a kind face filled with furrows. She wore a red top with a yellow flower pattern and had a bandage on her left elbow.

"May I ask what happened to your arm?" I asked.

"I fell a few days ago. I got dizzy and lost balance. It was a bad day. I was out searching for my cellphone because some *malandro* stole it while I slept." she responded.

"I'm sorry to hear that."

"It's all good now", she said calmly.

"Did you get your phone back?" I asked.

"No. But my friend Lillie lets me borrow hers, so I'm in touch with my family," replied Doña Natividad.

"Did Lillie come to Tijuana with you?"

"No! We met here. We share a tent now. We look out for each other. Anyhow, you may take my photo if you wish, but you know how it goes..." she said with a smile as she rubbed her index finger and thumb together in the universal sign for money.

"Naturally, Doña Natividad. But I'd like to hear your story first."

"Ha! How much time do you have? I'm seventy-three! You want my whole story?" she said amusingly with jittery gestures.

Other migrants started to gather around her; she seemed to be the life of the party. I explained to Doña Natividad that I was there to hear the migrant's stories and their impressions of the new U.S. government.

"Beh!" she said. "I think people here are dreaming up all sorts of outcomes. I don't think anybody knows with any certainty what's going to happen."

"So why are you here?" I asked.

"I'm actually saving a spot for my granddaughter", she responded. "Once she shows up with my daughter, my daughter and I will go back to Tuxtla Gutiérrez."

"Wait, wait, wait; your grandchild is going to cross alone?" I asked baffled.

"No, she will cross with her babies," she responded.

"Wait, wait, wait, wait... How old is your grandchild?"

"Twenty-two." Doña Natividad responded with a puzzled look. "What's so hard to understand, güero?" she said holding out her hands. The migrants around her laughed at the old woman's histrionic ways, and I couldn't help but let out a chuckle either.

"Nothing; it's just I imagined a child when you mentioned your grandchildren. You don't look that old, is what I'm saying," I asserted.

"Ha! I am filled with life, like a big old oak tree," she said clenching her fists and puffing her chest. The audience of migrants, which grew as the minutes passed, let out a hearty laugh.

"Okay, I get it now. We are talking four generations here. You, Doña Natividad, are the great-grandmother."

"Correct," she replied.

"And you're keeping a spot here you say?"

"Okay, *amigo*," she said showing me the palm of her hand. "Let me tell you my story from the moment I get out of Honduras."

Doña Natividad was born and raised in Yoro, but lived most of her life in Chamalecón, in the outskirts of San Pedro Sula.

"I had a little store there, a *pulpería*, and the mara-18 started extorting me", she explained. "At one point, they basically asked me to simply hand over the store, and my tiny apartment above it. They had killed many people in the neighborhood already, so I wasn't about to argue with them. So I just left. What was I to do?" she looked at her audience, the rhetorical question lingering in the air as they watched in silence.

"I'm an old woman," Doña Natividad went on. "I have worked hard. I have been kind. I deserve a godly death. *Una muerte de Dios.*" she said with aplomb.

"What do you mean by a 'godly death'?" I asked.

"It's when you die in peace, content, and you die because God calls you to his side," she explained. "Not because some *malandro* shoots you in the street like a dog! I'm telling you; they were killing people over a couple pesos…"

143

Doña Natividad and her daughter crossed Honduras' border into Guatemala, and then Guatemala's border into Mexico. After many months of dense paperwork, she was able to become a resident in Mexico.

"At the beginning, my idea was to keep going north to reach the U.S. But I'm an old woman. I had stayed in Tuxtla Gutierrez while my Mexican papers came out, and before I knew it, I was quite comfortable there. I worked as a street sweeper and had my own rental room. I decided to stay there, in the state of Chiapas".

Things changed when Doña Natividad's granddaughter, Suyapa, lost everything in Honduras when the back-to-back hurricanes Eta and Iota destroyed her home and her livelihood.

"My granddaughter Suyapa really suffered last year. She was able to move away to a more peaceful area with no gang violence... Only to be hit by the pandemic and the hurricanes. So, when this Biden guy wins, she says; *"This is it, I'm leaving Honduras"*.

Upon arriving in Mexico, Suyapa and her two babies were held up in a migration facility that served two purposes; the first was to ensure they did a proper quarantine; the second was to process the paperwork necessary to travel through the country legally.

"Now, after the pandemic and the hurricanes, everybody and their mother wants to go see this Biden guy", Doña Natividad narrated. "So Mexico is making it a little bit harder for Hondurans, 'cause we just keep showing up at the south!"

It was a curious turn of events; for some reason, while the Remain in Mexico program was in full force, Mexico had been keen to receive migrants. Now that the border cities were once again filling up with makeshift camps of hopeful nomads, Mexico didn't seem so interested in helping the migrants along, as they figured they weren't entering the country with the right mindset. After all, there is a big difference between moving to a new city to settle in and work; and doing it to camp out in the street awaiting a signal from the U.S. that may never come. Thus, Mexico devoted less and less resources to migrants and made the Mexican immigration paperwork more tiresome. Of course, the pandemic added another level of difficulty to the whole ordeal, or, at least, an excuse to deal with matters with a reduced sense of diligence. As Suyapa's detention in the south dragged on and other migrants started camping at the northern border, Doña Natividad felt the urge to travel northbound by herself in order to save a spot for her grandchild.

"You'd think my daughter would have made the trip up here instead of me, huh? But no, my *hija* has hypertension and some other health issues, whereas I... well, you know, I'm strong as an oak tree!" she said nudging me. "It was my job as a mother to protect her. I told her, '*mija*, I will go to Tijuana to pave the way for Suyapita'. And so here I've been for the past five weeks. If they do open up the U.S. for migrants, I want to make sure my Suyapita can make it. It's important that she is here among the first migrants. That's why I came," she said with gravity. "I know very well this is my last big trip. After this, I'm going to go back to Tuxtla Gutiérrez, save up and buy a few hens and wait for my godly death," she said with a longing smile.

"Don't you want to cross to the U.S. as well?" I asked.

"Me? No!" she said as she shook her head. "What for? I'm old, I've lived my life. I don't have time for the American dream... I wouldn't want to take someone else's spot," she declared earnestly. "Besides, I've heard what it's like; man and woman need to work two jobs each to make a living there. You need not one, but two cars! You need your own washing machine! Rooms are expensive! It's just too complicated!" she clamored, much to the amusement of her fellow migrants. "And while we're on the subject; Tijuana is expensive too! I don't know who they think they are here, 'cause this is still Mexico!" she said pointing at the ground beneath her feet with an attitude.

The crowd around her laughed and also validated her insight with comments like *'She's right, you know'*, *'That is true'*.

"Doña Natividad, you're a good comedian; you make uncomfortable truths hilarious" I told her.

"Naaah. I'm just a street sweeper. And so I shall remain once I get back to Tuxtla Gutiérrez, Chiapas," she declared with a dignified air of self-importance.

"How much is a hen?" I asked her.

"The egg-laying kind, about 60 pesos, I suppose", she estimated. "Why?"

"That should buy you a few", I told her as I handed her some money. "Now, let's get your portrait, you beautiful old oak tree."

7. Contentment.

The pandemic changed everyday life as we knew it. We didn't go out much and we weren't receiving visits at home. Our three-year-old girl's school year was truncated. The days at home became a chaotic improvisation to get things done and keep our girl mildly entertained –and educated. It didn't take us long to realize that we needed help. Before the pandemic, we usually received the aid of a cleaning lady twice a week. That ended once we decided we couldn't have people coming and going from our house with the viral storm unfolding outside; we needed somebody who would live with us and aid us in our daily chores. Before the pandemic, I had always been reluctant to this idea. For one thing, I wasn't thrilled about inviting a total stranger to move in with the family. I also considered it to be a luxury that, I feared, would make us lose touch with reality. The pandemic put an end to such opinions, as the luxury suddenly appeared to be a vital necessity to keep the home afloat.

We met Yuliza, as usually happens with these matters, through the referral of another cleaning lady from the neighborhood. These chains of acquaintance are the de facto labor pool of thousands of migrants from southern Mexico; a worker already settled in Tijuana recommends a friend, schoolmate, or cousin from their hometown usually in the rural areas of the more impoverished states (Chiapas, Oaxaca, Puebla, Guerrero...). A phone interview later, the recommendee is on a flight to Tijuana. Yuliza hailed from San Francisco Cabayua, a remote mountain village in the state Oaxaca. She was a petite twenty-something year old with a swarthy complexion and a beaming white smile. Demure at first, she took a few days to reveal her radiantly joyous nature, helped in no small part by the endless shenanigans and remarks of our three-year-old daughter Isabel, who was perennially intrigued by Yuli's Oaxacan background: her ranch, her large family, her crops, her language, her animals... For the ears of a young girl, Yuli's evocations seemed like a world out of a fairy tale; a small village in a mountainous valley, with no more than two hundred people and no cars, paved roads, malls, nor movie theaters. Just clean air, fields, animals, wood fired meals, and days to fill with no time wasted on city disturbances.

"Yuli", Isa asked. "Is it true you have horses?"

"Yes. We have two".

"Are you rich? Mom says horses are expensive..."

Yuli would giggle at such remarks and give mom and dad a nervous glance that seemed to say *"Should I reply to that? Better yet, can I reply to that convincingly?"* For what to say to a young child's perfectly implacable logic? Horses, we had told her, were very high maintenance animals that demanded a lot of costly care –only princesses with lots of wealth could afford them. If Yuli had horses, then it stood to reason that she must be some sort of royalty.

"You see, *hija*, Yuli's horses actually work for Yuli", my wife explained. "They're not pets. She has them to help her family on the field."

Yuli nodded and added. "They also carry us to places, because we don't have a car".

"Why don't you have a car, Yuli? Cars are faster than horses. And you can play music in them. You can't play music on a horse," she pointed out.

Yuli laughed heartily before contending Isa's remark.

"Yes, you can! I ride my horse with my headphones on all the time. It's the same as if it had its own radio."

"No", replied my daughter "It's not the same, because a horse doesn't have any buttons."

"That is true", Yuli granted with a titter.

My daughter's fixation with Yuli's world extended onto the linguistic realm; whenever Yuli was on the phone with someone from back home, the curious child would press her ear against Yuli's bedroom door.

"Yuli! Yuli! Is that English?" she would pry.

Yuli would laugh from the other side, before sticking her head out.

"No. It's mixteco. I don't speak English."

"Mmmh."

"Leave Yuli alone! She's on the phone, can't you see?" I told Isa.

Yuli would withdraw into her room once more, waving goodbye.

"Yuli, wait! You have to teach me Mixteco later, okay?" my daughter requested.

"You got it!" Yuli giggled.

The Mixteco lessons would usually unfold over the dinner table. Isa would point to various objects around her and demand to know their equivalent prehispanic word.

"How do you say water?"

"Water is *n'ducha.*"

"Tortilla?"

"*Dita.*"

"Tomato?"

"*Te nana*", Yuli replied with an ingratiating smile. It seemed as if Isa's interrogation wasn't aimed at learning, precisely, but at shooting the breeze with inane conversation to put off having to eat her veggies.

"Isa", I told her. "Eat your food and stop quizzing Yuli. Let her eat in peace."

"You should try to retain one word, and ask her to teach you another tomorrow," my wife added.

Isa looked at us defiantly before sinking her fork into her tomato and holding it up.

"*Te nana*", she muttered solemnly before devouring it.

※

This was not Yuli's first time in Tijuana. She had been once before, also holding a job as a housekeeper. It was common for young women from Oaxaca to make this sort of incursion into big cities and work stints ranging from a few months to a couple of years, before returning home. Any given Sunday at any Tijuana mall, you would find posses of ladies from Southern Mexico enjoying their day off, their indigenous languages gracing the weekend ambience. They were a tight community, always ready to recommend one another for a new job should one find their current situation to be exploitative; many had to put up with grueling schedules, bratty children, night shifts to tend to newborn babies (while the parents carried on sleeping!) and being accused of theft when things went missing in chaotic households. Sadly, such occurrences were common, and for these girls there was nowhere to turn; no human resources department, no contract to lean on, no nothing. Most housekeeper jobs were strictly under the table, leading to black market economies that the government had never truly been able to regulate –and not for the lack of trying. The free market always won out, however, as much of the proposed legislation made the hiring of these workers cost prohibitive. Still, the young women took their chances when finding the houses that would effectively become their homes for substantial chunks of their lives. The pay was substantially higher than just about any job they'd find back home, and the opportunity afforded them the chance to check out the city life that was so different from their country backgrounds. Of course, there was always the option of working in the city's *maquilas* (textile factories and assembly lines). Though the schedules there could be less chaotic and the job better protected by law, most women preferred to work in homes as opposed to in big industrial complexes; these were usually located in the outskirts of the city, known to be especially dangerous, and particularly so for women. Besides, enduring long shifts inside a dimly lit industrial complex, packed with noise, harmful chemicals and safety hazards, was not exactly an enticing prospect, especially if the alternative was trying to land a warm and loving family for which to work as a housekeeper. If the families took a chance when welcoming a stranger to the home, the housekeeper's insertion into that home was no less a leap of faith. This wasn't a job where you could simply storm out of the office at the end of the week and forget about your exasperating boss for a couple of days. My wife and I went to great lengths to make sure Yuli felt comfortable and at ease in our home, always keeping track of her workload so as not to overwhelm her. Besides, there were other aesthetic changes that had to happen in the house in order to make her feel welcome.

"No more swearing," my wife reminded me. "No more walking around in your underwear either."

Soon after she arrived, (and after a few days of quarantine) Yuli started opening up and confessed that she has happy working with us. The pandemic had made the house particularly chaotic, as we had to find ways to keep our children entertained and happy within the confines of those walls. Despite the jumbled and disrupted flow of the home, Yuli found this ambience preferable to her previous work in Tijuana.

"The woman I used to work with would host lots of parties", she told us. "Late at night, when the guests had finally gone, she would pretty much demand that I carry her to her bedroom -she ended up pretty drunk! And then I'd be expected to wash the dishes well into the wee hours of the night, so that in the morning it would be as if there had been no celebration the night before."

"Well," my wife replied. "You won't see any of that here. The only drinking problem in this house is Isabel spilling her chocolate milk."

For the first few weeks, we asked Yuli to refrain from going out on her days off, as the virus wreaked havoc through the city. We didn't feel great about this, as it was not much of a day off if she was asked to stay in the home. As weeks passed, we started to venture outside a little more, slowly getting used to everyday life with the viral particles roaming in the air. She started to arrange get-togethers with her friends. Her usual plan was to meet in the park and take a leisurely stroll to their favorite taco joint. Then, they'd go shopping to a nearby open-air mall.

"How do you like Tijuana, Yuli?" I asked her once as I drove her through the city to own of her meetups.

"It's... It's fine, I guess", she said almost lethargically.

"Come on, now. I'm not from here. You can be honest. I think it's a damn ugly city", I told her.

She laughed and let out a resigned sigh.

"Yeah, but... Really, the thing I don't like about it is that you *always* need money to live in a place like this."

I must have frowned at the remark, not knowing what to make of it; was she being naïve or incredibly profound? She caught my surprised look and went on to explain.

"Well, what I mean is; I'm not used to needing money *every day*. In my *pueblo*, I'll need some from time to time, but generally we don't *need* to buy stuff. The irony is that the city is supposed to present you with new opportunities, new blessings. But really, it also makes you so much more dependent. You always *need* to buy things. You always *need* to pay bills. You have to make more money so you can *afford* to live in the city".

"Wait, what do you mean you don't buy things in Oaxaca?" I asked.

"We do, of course we do. Just only the things we don't make ourselves; little things that you'd use every day like... toothpaste, or soap. But otherwise, we make our own tortillas, grow beans and other vegetables, have a few hens for eggs, streams and wells for water..."

"What about fish, or red meat?"

"We don't have them. But... that's what I am saying; we don't really *need* them. We have enough food with the things we grow."

I liked that philosophy. After all, how many things do we start to *need* only after we realize we don't have them? The false sense of necessity arises only after we convince ourselves we are missing out. But before that, we make do with what there is, and that is that. Therein lies the difference between poverty and misery; a person may be poor in material terms, living much more meagerly than what is considered normal. In misery, however, that lack of means translates to an exacerbated feeling of abject exclusion and despair. Perhaps, I told myself, it's a mistake to assume all poor people are miserable, just as it is a mistake to assume people who are well off cannot be miserable themselves. It's all about contentment. And yet, that plainly stated distinction still seemed to simplify an extremely nuanced and complex reality. There is, after all, a difference between *choosing* to live in poverty and having to do it because you have no other option. Is this lack of choice what ends up constituting that placid, or dare I say *resigned* contentment? Or is it not the lack of choice, but the absolute inexperience of other ways of life deemed more modern and pleasant that makes the extreme frugality of the rural life bearable? They say ignorance is bliss. However, for one, Yuli had experienced the vibrant and progressive dynamism of Tijuana for some time now, and she seemed mostly unimpressed, or at least, unconvinced that the city life was worth it, after factoring in all of its demands.

"You know what's ironic, Yuli? Now minimalism is becoming a trend. Many people are getting rid of as many things as they can. They have reached the conclusion that having so many things doesn't make one happy. It's just distracting noise. Also, city folks are starting to grow their own vegetables, bake their own bread, make their own cheese, things like that. The pandemic has urged people to become more self-sufficient. It's almost as if people in cities wish they lived like in a rural village like yours."

"And people from villages like mine want to go to the city", Yuli laughed.

"Well, we all romanticize what we don't have. Life in your village does sounds pretty... idyllic", I told her. "So why come here?"

"It gets pretty boring in my village", she admitted. "I like going away just long enough to start to miss it. Then go back. Then get bored and leave again", she said with a guilty laugh. "I know it makes no sense".

"No, no; it does make sense", I told her. "You're looking for a balance. We all want to have the right amount of all that is good; family, friends, health, opportunity... And sometimes you can't have it all at once in the same place. So you go back and forth between two places, between two worlds. But it's like trying to balance a seesaw by yourself; you can dart from one end to the other, but more often than not you'll be touching the ground."

"That's what it is", she said pensively.

"But Yuli", I told her "You're young. You aren't married and you have no children. Nothing is tying you down. No move you make is final. You can choose to live off the land in your little village, or work in Tijuana cleaning houses... or do something entirely different."

"You're firing me already?" she asked kiddingly with a nervous grin.

"Not at all!" I assured her. "We love your help and your company. But... we'd be happy to see you pursue something more."

"I don't know..." she said, and an awkward silence followed.

I wanted to remind her she was smart and capable, and that she had her whole life ahead of her. I wanted to tell her she should consider some form of higher education to get in a line of work that was more lucrative and less extenuating. But for some reason, pushing that message seemed odd coming from me –at the end of the day, I was just another confused migrant looking for a definitive sense of belonging. Besides, I figured the advice would come across as patronizing –especially from a person barely a few years older. Furthermore, I had become something of a relativist when it came to judging the validity and cogency of conventional paths of life, because mine up to that point had been anything but conventional. At the end of the day, people just want to be happy. The level of sophistication or simplicity with which we all aim to reach that goal is –or should be- purely a matter of personal preference. I respected the life choices of the overworked-entrepreneur-turned-millionaire-CEO, the schoolteacher with the long summer holidays, and the humble farmer who lived only off the bounty of his orchard. Though their means may vary, there's no doubt that all three can achieve happiness or fall prey to despair and sorrow.

And yet, I had the nagging sense that I could contribute my small grain of sand to fighting one of Mexico's biggest problems; the lack of social mobility. Mexico still functioned with the momentum of centuries of feudalism, and the folks in the lower rungs of the social pyramid tended to remain there from one generation to the next. This was particularly true for the disenfranchised rural areas in the southern states, such as Yuli's

Oaxaca. However, I truly felt a healthy and robust middle class could finally be achieved in Mexico. I believed strongly that the internet had democratized education and that education was the ultimate tool with which to become more prosperous and independent. I myself had learned new skills online to advance my professional aspirations and accomplishments. Education was there for the taking, but some people still hadn't been told.

"Look;" I said to her, "the whole world has been resorting to online classes because of the pandemic. There are free courses on just about anything. You should check it out! If there is something that you want to learn about, just let us know. I'd be happy to lend you my laptop, and we can work on a schedule that makes sense."

Yuli smiled timidly but said nothing.

"I know I'm not your father, so... forgive me if I speak out of place. I'm not pressuring you or anything. What I mean is; if in ten years' time you're still cleaning homes, I just hope it's because it's what you truly want to be doing. You're indeed great at it. So I've the feeling you'd be great at a whole lot of other things. You're young, you have time; these are the years to explore and keep on learning. There's something out there that I'm sure would make your heart sing!"

Yuli's eyes welled up and I felt guilty for having started such an existentialist conversation with the housekeeper. We arrived at the park where she was to meet her friends. She put on her antiviral mask and stepped out of the car.

"Thank you", she said.

～◡～

A few short weeks later we found out Yuli's birthday was approaching. After much poking and prying, my wife and I finally discovered what Yuli would like for her birthday.

"I'd love a basic knitting kit. I've been watching a lot of tutorials online, and I'd love to try it out", she said timidly.

"Say no more!" I responded.

We bought Yuliza a basic knitting kit, and after a few short days she had already fashioned several winter hats and used up all the yarn. I asked her if she wanted to keep learning that craft, to which she responded with an enthusiastic 'yes', and I told her I'd be happy to buy her more yarn so she could keep practicing. Meanwhile, my wife had posted the hats on group chats with local friends, and soon the fuzzy confections began to garner the interest of potential buyers. Tijuana had a dynamic economy of entrepreneurs and hustlers who pushed their products and services through social media. This digital marketplace had only increased with the pandemic, as many people had lost their jobs and were doubling down on their hobbies and passions to try to make a profitable side hustle of them. Homemade candles and soaps, cooked meals, curated secondhand clothing, and handmade accessories were among the many things sold and traded in this modern-day forum. Yuli saw the potential and used her free time to crank up production.

"I may have gotten carried away", I told her as I emptied a big bag full of yarn balls on the coach. Yuli giggled nervously.

"That's a lot of yarn!" she said.

"You're making a lot of hats!" I replied. "You can try making a blanket too!"

Yuli inspected her new yarn stock, which was diverse beyond anything she'd seen before. I had tried to provide her with a versatile range of lively colors. One yarn ball gradually changed pastel colors along the thread. Another skein had the particularity of being glittery. I also brought her a couple that were of a slightly thicker thread.

"These are good for scarves", I told her.

"Where did you get all these?" she asked me.

"San Diego. They have so much of everything in the U.S." I responded.

"Wow...!"

Yuli had never set foot in the U.S. Every day, she saw the neighboring country from the house, as the empty hills of San Ysidro, right behind the border wall, were clearly visible from our balcony. Often, as she stepped outside to hang up laundry, I saw her take a few seconds to stare into the distance.

"It's like all of Tijuana's madness stops right there and it's all quiet and peaceful on the other side", she reflected.

"Mmmh. It can get pretty mad over there too", I told her.

Yuli entertained the dream of moving to the U.S., as so many relatives and friends had done before her. When she was growing up, her father had lived and worked in the U.S. as an undocumented migrant. She didn't see him for nine years, but it was his father's sacrifice abroad that ensured Yuli could finish high school, while other teenagers around her were being pulled out of school to start working in the fields. Her father had since returned, with very impoverished health after years of working physically taxing jobs and neglecting paying the doctor a visit. Yuli confessed that her main motivation for leaving her home in Oaxaca was to save up to give her father proper medical attention. Thus, the migratory flows perpetuated one generation after the next, each looking to improve the life of the folks left back home.

Every now and again, Yuli joked about leaving Tijuana and moving to the U.S. She had a sister living in Wisconsin, and she figured she could follow in her footsteps. Said footsteps would have Yuli sneak into American territory using obscure and dangerous passages through the borderline in remote regions where there was no wall. This type of plan always called for the expensive services of a coyote, that is, the person who would guide the illegal migrants through the empty deserts of Southern U.S. territory.

"My sister did it. I have another two friends from my pueblo who recently did it too", Yuli said. My wife and I showed startled aversion to any sort of plan like that, and Yuli giggled at our dismayed reactions.

"Yuli, that sounds very shady. And expensive. You don't want to have a debt with certain types of people..." I told her.

～～～

One night, Yuli came to us after dinner, as we were getting ready to go to bed. She had her hands formally crossed across her waist and showed a serious and slightly nervous demeanor.

"*Señor, señora*: I have a big favor to ask." Yuli said timorously. "My cousin was caught by border patrol trying to sneak into *Los Estados*. He's a minor so he can't go on a plane back to Oaxaca unaccompanied by a family member."

My wife and I listened intently.

"My question to you is: could you book my uncle a flight to go and get him? My cousin is currently being held in some jail cell in Juarez," she explained.

"And your uncle can bail him out of there?" I asked.

"Yes. He just needs to get there as soon as possible" Yuli explained. "It's a week by bus from Oaxaca, and considering meals and all, the plane is faster and cheaper. My uncle just doesn't have internet to book the flight himself. He would need to go to the Oaxaca airport just to book the flight, which is four hours by bus from our pueblo... He'd prefer to book it as soon as possible."

"I see", said my wife. "We'll help you."

"I'll pay you back in full right now" said Yuli.

"Of couse, Yuli. But my question is: will your uncle pay *you* back?" my wife asked.

Yuli shrugged her shoulders and smiled nervously.

"I'll figure it out with him", she said.

"Heck, you should get your cousin to pay you back!" I suggested.

"Ha! He's like fifteen, and I'm sure he has absolutely no money left now that's he has tried to emigrate", Yuli explained disappointedly. "Besides, he'll have to pay back the loan he got to travel to the U.S..."

"What a predicament..." I sighed.

"I imagine it's a lot of money... How will he pay for it all?" my wife asked.

Yuli snorted.

"I suppose he'll have to find a good job... Once he gets to the U.S."

She spoke very casually of the expensive and life-threatening exodus undocumented migrants made to the U.S. She mentioned the dynamic of getting caught and trying again with stoic resolve, arguing that few people make it the first time, as it is a game of trial and error. But I had the strong feeling her casual confidence didn't do justice to a process that was much more easily said than done.

"I pray you never try it, Yuli," I said, putting my hands together and hoping she'd sense the serious intent in my jocular tone.

Yuli giggled. She knew her flippant comments in which she entertained the idea of becoming a *mojado* were bound to shock my wife and I. Every now and again, she'd crack a casual joke to elicit a scandalized reaction from us. But, as we say in Spanish; *"Entre broma y broma, la verdad se asoma" ("Between one joke and the next, the truth peeks out").* Yuli seemed somewhat blasé about Tijuana, but the American dream did appear to entice her enough to consider a humiliating and dangerous journey into the perilous desert. Needless to say, she was not alone.

PART THREE

Elegy for the fallen migrant

1. The desert.

"Look", said Don Ely. "Why don't you come with us? I'm not such a fan of giving interviews. I prefer it when our work speaks for itself".

"Oh, I'd love to check it out in person", I told him on the phone. "I just assumed you didn't let outsiders join you. I imagine it's dangerous."

"Well… can you walk long distances?"

"Define long."

"We have done fifteen, eighteen miles in a day, something like that".

"This pandemic has made me a little soft, but I'd like to think I'll be fine."

Don Ely laughed on the other end of the line.

"Okay… Just bring proper hiking boots, no trainers or anything like that."

"Sounds good. But what I meant by dangerous is… doesn't it get awfully hot our there?"

"Yes, but not so much this time of year."

"And… what about… shootouts, cartel violence, things like that?" I asked awkwardly, almost embarrassed. Was I just throwing a bunch of trite Hollywood clichés at him? After all, the few things I thought I knew about life in the Sonoran Desert I had picked up from the movies. Don Ely paused for a second.

"Mmh… Nah… I think we'll be fine," he explained. "Where we are going is a military base. The U.S. army uses the desert for drills. The danger may be finding an unexploded bomb from a jetfighter. It's happened in the past. We just report them and steer clear. The soldiers take care of it after we leave."

"So… no narco violence?" I asked nervously.

"It's never happened to us. Not in that area."

"Okay… Let me check with my wife. But I'd love to go."

The pitch to my wife didn't go swimmingly. She wasn't thrilled about the idea of me leaving for a weekend to join volunteer search and rescue group in the inhospitable Arizona desert. I argued I wanted to see it up close, as some issues cannot be fully comprehended if they haven't been experienced first-hand. Besides, joining a bunch of expert desert dwellers sounded tremendously exciting.

"You make it sound like you're going to summer camp. But it's not that" she said with a grave tone. "You'll probably see some very ugly things out there."

"I'm aware." I assured her, although I later realized I was not. My wife's words were ratified soon after, when I spoke to Don Ely on the phone again:

"We've got word of a missing migrant, and some likely coordinates", he announced. "We're organizing a search party for this weekend, in case you want to join us."

"I will go", I said, determined. "Just one question; how can you afford to wait until the weekend? How can you be sure the guy will live that long?"

"Oh… Just to be clear; we're looking for his corpse. He went missing last September."

We were in March.

"I see…" I responded, trying to appear unfazed.

"In fact, we already looked for him in September and didn't find him. What happened is, another migrant who recently crossed happened to pass by his remains in the desert and checked his wallet to identify him. He reached out to us and gave us word. But the poor soul has been on our list for months...," said Don Ely. "So hopefully we can find him and make sure he goes home to receive a proper burial. Does that sound good?"

"Yes. I'll be there".

~~~

A volunteer named Octavio picked me up in San Diego. He was a stocky short man in his fifties with a pencil moustache and drove a black pickup truck with the logo and name of the organization: *Águilas del Desierto (Desert Eagles)*. Upon getting in the vehicle, Octavio shook my hand and said:

"How do you feel about dead people?"

"Um..."

I was startled by such an odd question, and before I could reply, he went on to explain.

"I've been tasked with picking up the ashes of a man from Querétaro, where I'm from. He died alone in the States. Diabetes. You know us, *la raza;* we don't like going to the doctor...." he said with a disappointed tone. "Anyway, a distant relative of his in México reached out to me to help him with the cremation. You see, I have a Facebook group; *'Migrants from the state of Querétaro'*. It has over a thousand members. That's where I got people to pitch in for the expenses. It's over $3,000 to be turned to ashes. Pricey, but way cheaper than sending over the whole body", he said. Then there was a pause.

"Many migrants are all alone here in this country, you see. Many die alone. We bond together as a community for this sort of thing. I hope you don't mind driving with the ashes in the trunk."

"No, that's fine."

We stopped at a funeral parlor in a shopping plaza in El Cajon. I sat in the lobby as Octavio took care of paperwork in the office. A wake was being held in the adjacent room, a chapel you could look into through large glass panels. In the open casket was a man in his sixties, peacefully laid down in an elegant suit with his hands across with chest. I observed quietly as family members approached him one by one to show their respects.

"Look at him," Octavio said, appearing behind me. "Old, elegant, peaceful... He looks like he's sleeping. That's the way to go. A far cry from the ones we see in the desert..." He did the sign of the cross, then showed me the bag he had been given with the ash urn in it. "We can go now".

"What was his name?" I asked, referring to the urn.

"Vicente. He was forty-nine. *Pinche diabetes...*"

We left El Cajon and directly merged into the Interstate 8 highway, which we followed eastbound for six hours. The mild Mediterranean scenery gave way to dry, rugged, mountainous landscapes as we approached inland California.

"I know these mountains well", said Octavio. "This is the way I came in over thirty years ago. *La Rumorosa."*, he said with melancholy.

La Rumorosa is the region between the border town of Tecate and the city of Mexicali. It is a treacherous terrain of strong winds and steep, rocky cliffs. Octavio explained that, back then, there was no border wall running through la Rumorosa, and one could sneak into the United States quite feasibly after an extenuating night hike over mountains.

"It was easy back then, almost fun, dare I say. If you got caught, they simply dropped you back in Mexico and you could try again straight away", he reminisced. "Heck, and then Ronald Reagan gave us amnesty and just like that I got my papers. Ha! How republicans have changed…!" he lamented.

As we drove parallel to the borderline, the infamous wall dipped in and out of sight through the jagged mountain range.

"*Pinche muro.* It's that damn wall", he said. "They pushed the migrants to the Sonora desert. There's no wall there, because they presumed the desert would act as a wall, a natural barrier, a deterrent of sorts. It goes to show they don't know how desperate a man can get. And that's how the desert turned into a manmade deathtrap."

Upon crossing the state line into Arizona, the topography plateaued into vast expanses of flat desert, with imposing elevations way in the horizon. At a little settlement called Gila Bend, we got off the 8 at a resting area to wait for other volunteers. They came one by one in beat-up SUV's. The sun was setting and the spotted clouds in the sky became all sorts of pink, golden and purple, floating over an endless arid blanket. The temperature was dropping fast, resulting in winds that howled like a tormented soul. Now, the scenery looked at once breathtakingly beautiful and eerily otherworldly.

"Welcome to the Sonora desert", said Octavio. "As beautiful as it is deadly."

After rendezvousing with the other volunteers, the caravan of six vehicles took another road, the 85, southbound. The sky was starry and the moon almost full. After forty-five minutes on the 85, at around midnight, we reached Ajo, a small ghost town made up of dirt roads, bungalows, old RV vans and a minimal main street with a dusty gas station and a dilapidated supermarket. There, we followed some barely marked dirt paths to the Águilas basecamp. The place consisted of about two acres of land on which stood a wooden ramada, (used for meeting, eating and such), two ramshackle construction trailers (for storage space and sleeping), and two portable restrooms. Around it, the settlement of Ajo and more desert as far as the eye could see, ever so dimly lit by the pale moonlight. As we unloaded the vehicles, a large man in his fifties approached me and reached out to shake my hand.

"Good to meet you in person. I'm Ely. Go get some rest, we get going in four hours."

<hr/>

I jolted awake when the 4x4's right side fell into a pronounced rut.

"Sorry," said Rubén at the wheel as he commanded his powerful vehicle out of the obstacle. It was dark. I must have slept less than three hours at the basecamp, where the night had been cold and winds loud like banshees made sleep very hard to reconcile.

We were driving through the desert right before dawn, the orange glow of the sun timidly starting to peek out over the distant eastward mountains. "We still have a while to go. You can nap a bit more if you want."

As I rested my head on the window and tried to get some sleep, we drove past an old sign riddled with bullet holes. It read:

Travel Caution

Smuggling and illegal immigration

may be encountered in this area.

~~⚬~~

"We are looking for Victor Humberto Cabrera Montoya, from Guatemala" Don Ely briefed us.

We had driven an hour and a half into the desert through border patrol trails. The sun was barely rising when we reached our starting point and the searchers gathered around Don Ely to hear his instructions as they geared up. There was a ritualistic solemnity to this moment, which volunteers tended in silence and with utmost attention; rucksacks were filled with water bottles and high-energy snacks, heavy-duty hiking boots were laced up tightly, sunscreen was applied, walkie-talkies were calibrated, and maps were passed around. Two migrants carried white wooden crosses wedged between their backs and their backpacks, presumably to serve as makeshift tombstones for the forsaken migrants we might find. Meanwhile, Don Ely proceeded with today's case.

"Victor Humberto was ditched by his coyote because he couldn't keep walking; he was suffering too many leg cramps. This was almost half a year ago, so he's all bones now. On the day he went missing, he was wearing a black shirt with long sleeves, camouflage pants, and a blue backpack. His sneakers were either Puma or Adidas. May we find this young man and give his family the peace they deserve."

A short prayer followed, and we were off. The volunteers stretched into the desert to form a line with which to comb the enormous terrain. More volunteers had shown up during the night, and now we numbered about thirty. Each person stood about twenty meters from the next. The first and last volunteers had bright yellow flags tied to the ends of their hiking staffs, to mark the beginning and the end of the search party. Some volunteers (mostly the wives and daughters of the men in the line) stayed with Don Ely; they would help drive all the vehicles to the finishing point some twelve miles away.

When the line was stretched out, Don Ely formally announced the start of the search through his walkie-talkie. The idea was to advance in unison, paying close attention to our surroundings, probing every shrub, descending into every dried-up riverbed and inspecting under every mesquite that could provide some shelter from the blistering sun.

"It's important to look in places with a bit of shade. That's usually where we find them", explained Doña Maricela, (Don Ely's wife) as she walked beside me. "The exhausted migrants stop to rest, sometimes taking naps from which they never wake up."

"Have you ever found remains out in the open, that is, not in a spot with shade?" I asked her.

"It's not common, but it happens. Those are the folks that lose their minds on account of the heat, the dehydration, all of that.

They wander aimlessly, frantically, delirious, and drop dead in any random place", she said dryly.

"I wonder which is worse", I thought out loud.

"I think I'd rather lose my mind", said Rubén, the volunteer advancing on the other side of Doña Maricela. I thought about it and came to the conclusion that I agreed with him. There must be some solace in dying after the desert has deprived you of your sanity and your conscience. Is a broken mind able to process the heavy significance of nearing one's end? Does the noise of a demented brain remove you from the suffering brought on by excruciating physical agony? Would a person in that state suffer the existentialist despair of staring at death in the eyes?

"I'd rather not think about it", Doña Maricela pitched in. "I can't imagine how dying insane is desirable in any circumstance. There have been cases of people running to hug saguaros to end their lives. The desert will do that to you... It's not pretty."

The saguaros were the towering cacti that peppered the Sonoran Desert. I had never seen them up close and always imagined they stood a little taller than an average person. In fact, most saguaros we were passing easily cleared the ten-meter mark.

"Pinches saguaros", reflected Rubén during the hike. "Those things could save the migrants' lives. Look at them! So stiff, so robust! That's because they're filled with water!"

Rubén, a Mexican living in Chandler, Arizona, earned a living as a landscapist. He explained how he was routinely hired to cut down saguaros in people's gardens.

"The thing about saguaros is that they don't have deep roots, but they grow very tall and very heavy. When they're old and big, a strong wind can topple them over. Those things weigh over a ton! Imagine the damage they can go if they fall on a house, a car, or –God forbid- a person...” he explained. “And those damn prickles -*no manches!* So they're good business; we charge about $2,000 to cut down a single saguaro. Let me tell you, when we go in there with a chainsaw, we end up drenched. They're filled with water! If only the poor migrants knew how to extract it...”

But most migrants didn't know the first thing about survival in the desert. Dehydration was perhaps the biggest obstacle they faced when attempting this deadly exodus. It was physically impossible to carry with them all the water they would need, as they could easily take as long as eight days to cover the eighty-something miles from the border to the Interstate 8, -the point where the *levantón* usually happens. *Levantón* means ‘pickup’ and refers to the moment the migrants and the coyote are swiftly picked up at a roadside and driven to a safe house. The migrants usually started their journey from Sonoyta, a small border town that over the years had become a wretched hive of organized crime. Sonoyta sits in the middle of the Sonoran Desert, and functions as the base of operations for the coyotes working in the region.

A little over ten years ago, a coyote would charge around $1,500 to cross a migrant. However, this line of work had become more and more lucrative over the years, as the border became more guarded and the penalties for human trafficking became more substantial. It used to be that, if a coyote was caught, he and the migrants he was guiding were simply deported at the border. Now, coyotes faced years of jail time in the U.S. before being deported. This had a tremendous effect on the profile of the typical coyote. They used to work solo, like freelancer desert guides with no ties to organized crime. They were people who knew the desert like the palm of their hands and could see to it that their clients crossed safely. But as the border became more and more impenetrable and the consequences for getting caught became more dire, it quickly became apparent that being a coyote could not be a one-man operation. It wasn't enough to be physically fit and to know the desert well. Now, a successful crossing was a logistical miracle. If border patrol was using the latest technology, so too were the coyotes; GPS, drones, radio, watchers perched in the surrounding mountains... All these elements had to play a part, causing significant overhead. That's when the cartels stepped in, offering their muscle, connections, and resources to get a piece of the lucrative human trafficking pie.

"So how much do the migrants pay the coyote?" I asked Doña Maricela as we traversed the desert.

"$8,000 was the last I heard. And the poor migrants take a loan to pay it, usually from rather shady creditors. Can you imagine? For that money, I'd just stay in Mexico and open a taco joint. The worst thing is when the migrants die in the desert, the widowed family still has to pay that debt..." she lamented.

"*Código siete, código siete!*", came a voice from her walkie-talkie. In the distance, Don Octavio was waving the yellow flag in the air.

"Did they find him?" I asked.

"No. But you should check it out", said Doña Maricela.

We walked over to find an old rucksack in tatters. A volunteer prodded it open with his staff and out fell countless flowers of weed, tightly bound in plastic wrap.

"That's 25kg of marijuana", said Doña Maricela. "Many migrants reach Sonoyta without any money, so this is how they pay their passage into the U.S. They do a delivery for the cartel."

"And they just dump the drugs here?"

"Well, it's a heavy load," said Don Octavio. "When push comes to shove, many migrants prefer to travel light and take their chances with the cartel, not with the desert."

The bag had begun to disintegrate under the sun, and Don Octavio guessed it had been there for many months.

"Alright, guys, let's step away and carry on with the search," said Doña Maricela.

"Do you jus leave the drugs lying there?" I asked.

"What, do you have any other ideas?" said another volunteer jokingly.

"No, what I mean is; don't you hand them over to the border patrol or something?"

"No", Doña Maricela explained. "There could be *halcones* watching."

Halcón is the Spanish word for falcon. The Sonoran Desert lingo to do with illegal crossings is like a menagerie of wild animals: first and foremost, there's the *coyote*, a moniker presumably explained by the animal's familiarity with the desert habitat. These are also called *polleros*, (something like *chicken handlers*), a metaphor perhaps to do with how the migrants trail behind the *pollero* like a line of baby chicks. Then there's the *burrero*; (the *donkeyman*); these are the poor migrants forced or paid to transport large bags filled with drugs across the desert (in English, a closely related term would be *mule*). The bag of drugs in front of us was left there by a *burrero*. And last but not least, there's the *halcones*. These are the watchmen strategically placed by the mafias way up on the surrounding mountains.

"They monitor every crossing with telescopes. If a migrant drops his load, they'll arrange to salvage the goods if they can. They're probably looking at us right now", explained Doña Maricela.

I looked around at the elevations in the distance. They appeared lifeless, indifferent, yet oddly spine-chilling.

"Besides, if border patrol sees us fidgeting with the drugs we bump into, we could have some serious explaining to do", Doña Maricela went on. "It's hard to get the permits to search these lands. Remember we are on military ground. If we want to keep obtaining permits in the future, we best behave. So when we see a bag of drugs like this, it's preferable to leave it alone and carry on."

Doña Maricela explained how in the early years of Águilas del Desierto, the military had always provided them with a companion to chaperone them in their incursions. After years of honest work and impeccable behavior, the volunteers of Águilas had earned the privilege of going on these desert hikes unsupervised.

"We want to keep it this way. In the past, if the soldiers tagged along, they immediately called border patrol whenever we came across a migrant. It was automatic deportation for them," Rubén explained.

"So what do you do now if you bump into a migrant?" I inquired.

"We give them food and water and ask them what they want to do. In these parts, they have likely been walking for over a week and are in pretty bad shape; dehydrated, malnourished, blistered feet, sunburnt, -the works," Doña Maricela said. "So we ask them what they want to do; most turn themselves in, and we call 911."

It was a case of Maslow's pyramid of needs at work. The migrants initiated their journeys enticed by ambitions goals of self-actualization, of achieving one's dreams and realizing their innermost potential. But out there on the hellish Sonoran Desert, the prospect of owning a big house, a lucrative business or a shiny Cadillac meant absolutely nothing when their most basic physiological needs were being neglected and their agonizing bodies started tormenting their minds with unbearable anguish. This was the point most migrants threw in the towel –if they got a chance to do so. But a brave few pressed on. Perhaps they weren't here for the mighty dollar. Perhaps what they left behind in their home countries really was worse than the Sonoran Desert. Perhaps, while persevering in the desert was probable death, returning home was a certain one.

"Not long ago, we came across a Salvadoran migrant who was in very bad shape but insisted he wanted to continue walking," Doña Maricela narrated. "We gave him food, water and bandages and respected his decision. We looked the other way as he staggered into the desert once more."

"We're all immigrants here; we cannot truncate the dreams of a fellow migrant, but we cannot carry them across the desert either," Don Octavio delineated.

This philosophy had been a point of contention in the past, when there had been instances of Águilas volunteers rebelling against the leaders when they refused to use their 4x4 trucks to get a migrant closer to his finish line. The migrant in question looked on the brink of death, but vehemently alleged he didn't want to give up the trek. Many among the volunteers guessed he must have perished soon thereafter.

"What we absolutely cannot do is give them a ride in our vehicles. The second we do that, we become coyotes ourselves", said Rubén.

~~~

Around six miles into the trek, my body started to resent the whole plan. With the sun was now blasting at full force and the desert laid endlessly before us in all directions, I started to get a glimpse of what the migrants endure. I had not worn my hiking boots in a mighty long time, and I realized I had never broken into them properly to begin with. A few hours in, I began to feel blisters forming beneath my toes. My back and shoulders also began to ache; I was carrying a heavy load of photographic gear as well as eight bottles of water (as instructed by Don Ely himself). I wasn't sure if these were the bottles we would need to drink during our hike, or if we were taking water in excess in case we ran into thirsty migrants.

"Take as many as you can", said Don Ely to me right before the party set out. "At this stage, the migrants have run out of water long ago…"

I asked him if the migrants did anything to prepare for the long days in the desert. Don Ely scoffed.

"No. No training, no nothing. They all come ill-prepared, with cheap, thin-soled sneakers." Don Ely lamented. Hours later, as my feet were beginning to scream in pain, I thought of all the migrants who covered much more ground than me, over many more days, with shoes that were much more inadequate than mine. The rest of their gear was equally lacking; they didn't carry enough protection from the sun, they never carried blankets thick enough to protect them from hypothermia in the cold nights, and of course they lacked sufficient rations of food.

"Once, we came upon a migrant who looked absolutely bone-weary", Rubén told me as we walked. "He carried with him an orange drink, so while more help arrived I told him: 'You can finish your Gatorade, we'll give you plenty of water for the way.' He looked at me and said: 'Gatorade? That's my piss...'"

I made a conscious effort to ignore the physical discomfort and focus on the breathtaking aesthetics of the desert. I had only ever seen such a landscape in Hollywood movies, in which the desert usually appeared with a grandiose monumental quality that somehow made it less menacing. I remembered an old Hollywood anecdote that posed a question I had often tossed around in my head; a very young Steven Spielberg visited a very old John Ford in his office. The budding filmmaker began to tell the veteran of his aspirations, but Ford cut him off saying: *"You see those three pictures of the desert on the wall? What's different about them?"* Spielberg analyzed them and responded that one had the horizon line closer to the top, another had it split the composition in even halves, and the third had the horizon line much closer to the bottom of the frame. *"And why do you think that is?"* asked Ford wryly. Spielberg admitted he didn't know. *"The day you figure out why you want to frame your horizon at the top, at the middle or at the bottom, then you'll be a good storyteller."*

I had often played back this exchange in my head, trying to figure out exactly what wisdom Ford was withholding from

Spielberg. As I advanced with the search party and I grew more and more tired, I found myself hanging my head low, seeing nothing but the dry gritty ground in front of me. I didn't want to acknowledge the long way ahead, so I kept my head low to simply focus on the next step, and then the next, and the next... I then understood that, in cinema, a horizon line that is close to the top and leaves most of the sky out of the frame conveys hardship, grief, and insurmountably adverse comeuppance. It is the view of somebody carrying a heavy load. On the other hand, a horizon line that cuts through the frame at the bottom translates to big, prodigious skies, -the sight of somebody looking up to the heavens in redemption, in bliss, in victory! It is the view of somebody who finally understands that, while the road traversed may have been long, it's nothing compared to the infinite expanse of salvation.

The landscape was so monotonous that the only references were the mountains in the horizon, but these were so far away that one could walk for an hour and get the sensation he was not advancing at all. The knee-high shrubbery also played its part in muddying any notion of progress, as at ground level, it was these plants that prevented us from seeing any of the few dirt paths marked in our maps. This desert foliage made the search difficult because it made it impossible to see any signs of migrants until we were in close proximity.

At one point, the dry soil under my foot gave way and I collapsed into an empty burrow, nearly spraining my ankle.

"Careful there!" yelped Rubén.

"Jeez, this terrain is treacherous!" I said as I composed myself. I looked around me and noticed the ground was riddled with similar holes, all made by animals that would rather be closer to hell than on the surface of the Sonoran Desert.

"You got lucky", said Rubén. "You could have landed on a rattlesnake!"

"Now imagine doing this hike in the dark, without as much as a flashlight. That's how the migrants do it", informed J.R., the only American volunteer in the search party.

"Seriously?" I asked in disbelief.

"Of course! During the day, they mostly hide from the sun and rest. They advance at night, when they cannot be spotted", he elaborated.

It was no wonder that so many migrants suffered foot injuries; they were walking on tremendously uneven ground without even the chance to see where they would set their foot next. It seemed like a metaphor for the immigration phenomenon at large, so filled with leaps of faith into the unknown.

"Yeah, man.... The shit these guys go through", J.R. sighed. "You know, Americans say the U.S. is in the dumps. Us white people like to complain about everything. But when I see the hell foreigners go through to get into the U.S., it makes me appreciate my country more."

I asked him how he came to join an organization made up almost entirely of Hispanic immigrants.

"I was hired to design the ramada at the basecamp", he explained. "I came down to Ajo from Flagstaff and helped to build it. Most of the volunteers are constructions workers, so we didn't hire any laborers for the project. I loved their camaraderie and their good humor. I don't understand them, but I love them", he laughed.

As I observed J.R. through the day, I got an idea of how limited his Spanish was. And yet he had developed a non-verbal shorthand with the whole group (who in turn spoke little to no English). J.R. was heavy built and tall, with a rosy skin tone that seemed to intensify in the heat. His big, weathered hands bore witness to the fact that, like the other volunteers, J.R. was a builder, a doer.

"I love Arizona, man," he said. "It's still like the wild west out here. Look around you", he said stretching his arms in awe. "There's plenty of room. And then people say the country is full... Bunch of bullshit."

Originally from Nebraska, J.R. explained how his family back home had taken to his newfound volunteering work.

"They're all like 'You go to the desert to do *what*?! Why would you help those criminals!?'" he said in an insufferable screechy tone. "So yeah, my parents think I'm a coyote on the weekends. There's just no nuance with some folks. It's crazy. But hey, they're my parents, and I love 'em," he said with a resigned smile.

As we plowed ahead, there were few signs of migrant activity. We found some clothes, a few winter blankets, and many empty water bottles.

"Why are the bottles all the same matte black?" I asked.

"The black blends in better with the earthy environment" Rubén explained. "Clear bottles can be spotted from far away, as they are bright and glisten."

"They look like repurposed detergent bottles or something," I said.

"You'd think so, but no; it's an actual bottled water brand they sell in Sonoyta", said Rubén.

Indeed, as I crouched to inspect the abandoned bottle in detail, I read the eroded tag: *Sun Water*. The words were written in a fun, summery typography. It was yet another disturbing sign of the cynical but extremely lucrative businesses blossoming in this deathly industry.

In other instances, our water bottle findings were more hope-inducing; gallons of water were scattered across the miles of arid wasteland, left there by other charity organizations with handwritten notes with messages like *"Almost there"* or *"Jesus loves you"*.

The line advanced, slowly but surely, and we neared the supposed coordinates where we may find Humberto: 32°39'15.8"N 112°25'20.6"W. Don Ely had triangulated this point based on the testimony of the migrant who saw Humberto's corpse. The group became more silent and focused as we reached that exact location. Any second now, any volunteer could stumble upon Humberto's remains.

The desert, in its irreconcilable amalgam of beauty and terror, also demanded solemnity and reverence for the fallen. The silence and the isolation were conducive to an atmosphere of deep introspection, not unlike the funeral home I found myself in the day before. There was something undeniably mystical about the desert, a powerfully immaterial quality that gave you the sense that there was a potent unseen realm at work there. These were, after all, the ancient lands of the Tohono O'odham indigenous peoples, whose ancestral mythology attributed sacred qualities to the awe-inspiring natural landscape. To this day, the Tohono O'odham tribe occupied much of the desert a few miles east of where we were conducting our search, where their reservation started.

For Don Francisco, the eldest man of the search party, the spirituality of the desert didn't derive so much from the beauty, scale and age of the place, but rather from the insurmountable number of horrifying deaths that had plagued the desert for hundreds of years. From the wars waged between the Native Americans and the U.S. government and the resulting diaspora of tribes through the smoldering barren land, to the Mexican and Central American migrant crisis of more recent years, the desert had claimed the lives of countless suffering souls.

"The place is *satanized*, I tell you", Don Francisco said with conviction. "There has been so much agonizing here. So much death. And, I'm sure, so much bargaining with the Devil to see you through when you're on your last legs", he said, looking at me deep in the eye. I must have not corresponded his level of gravitas, because he went on: "I'm serious, Spaniard! I have felt it! I'm walking along and suddenly something jolts my backpack. I fall to the ground and look around me... and there's nothing."

He also told me of his reservations about visiting an eerie mount called Cerro de la Aguja, one of the most inaccessible points of the region. Águilas del Desierto had carried out several searches there, as it was a stretch of the crossing where many migrants went missing. Most volunteers agreed that the place was haunted.

"That *cerro* is where the weirdest shit happens", Don Francisco explained. "Every time we go, there's some sort of unforeseen trouble. I'm telling you, it's like there's demon souls here sabotaging our work; they don't like that we locate the corpses and send them home. Those corpses are like sacrifices to the desert. Yes, the desert will carry to a new life, but a few shall remain behind to pay the passage of the others" Don Francisco unraveled his theory with a sinister twinkle in his eye. "The bodies are not ours to take... So, I kid you not, there's ghosts sabotaging our work here", he whispered. He also described a strange vibe in El Cerro de la Aguja, a heaviness in the air. "And that rock perched up on top of the mountain? If that isn't Death itself, looking down on all of us..."

"It's does look like Death," Doña Maricela agreed with a mischievous laugh, injecting a little levity into the conversation. She showed me a photograph on her cellphone, and there it was, clear as day; a darkened rock formation in the shape of an ominous cloaked figure, with creases and all.

"Do you think El Cerro de la Aguja is haunted?" I asked Doña Maricela.

"Who's to say. We have gone there in the summer, when it's over 120ºF. We've been known to get dizzy, disoriented, erratic even", she admitted.

"No, Doña Maricela; it's not the heat. It's something much darker, I'm sure", Don Francisco insisted.

"Well," said Doña Maricela "I always bring plenty of water and a rosary. Whatever it may be, it's good to have insurance".

"We found something," alerted a voice through the walkie-talkie. A cacophony of white noise, beeps and feedback followed as the other volunteers saturated the channel to respond.

"Over here!" came a voice lost in the distant shrubbery. As we walked in that general direction, I tried to ready myself for the ghastly sight of a real human corpse. I found some strange relief in the fact that, at this point, the elements must have reduced poor

Humberto to a skeleton. The harrowing process of decay, with its stomach-churning sights and putrid smells, must have concluded long ago. And yet I didn't want to let a lifeless heap of bleached bones remove me the fact that they were once a person, with dreams and fears like all of us, and a family back home who a few months back bid him farewell as he walked out the front door, looking to secure a better future in the land of dreams. Such were the thoughts running through my head as we neared the scene. I tried hard to retain a sense of respect for the forsaken migrant, reminding myself that if I were to come face to face with his remains, I'd be looking at an actual human being and not a Halloween prop.

"Somebody reached him before we did", said Don Octavio, who stood in front of a mesquite tree lined with yellow caution tape which marked a small perimeter. An old dusty baseball cap, washed out by the sun, and a thick blanket still remained lying on the ground.

It appeared some other organization had found Humberto in the days before and failed to communicate with Águilas del Desierto. We contrasted the coordinates as guessed by Don Ely with the ones corresponding to the very location we were on now. They matched closely enough, but some volunteers theorized that that couldn't possibly been have been Humberto's dying place.

"Whomever they found here hadn't been dead nearly as long as Humberto", Rubén speculated. "Look; there's no fat markings", said Rubén.

"What do you mean?" I asked.

"When a person dies, the body bloats after a few days; it's the gases accumulating as it decomposes", Rubén said. "Soon thereafter, bloody, fatty liquids ooze out and leave a dark stain on the ground. There's no stain here, so my guess is: whomever they picked up here had only been dead for up to three days", he concluded.

"But suppose all that you're describing happened half a year ago; would the stain remain to this day?" I asked.

"Oh, yeah. The stain lasts years", Rubén noted.

The volunteers spoke casually about the intricacies of the human corpse. It was clear that, despite the evident estimation they had for the migrants, they had grown insensitive to the sight of death. It wasn't a heartless type of callousness, but a stoic and resigned response to a horrible reality they could do nothing about.

"Isn't it difficult seeing all those corpses?" I asked them.

"You get used to it. It's never pretty, but you get used to it", said J.R.

"Strangely, the worst ones are the ones with no decay at all. We are certain we've come across migrants who died only a few hours, even moments, before we reached them. We get the feeling we could have saved them if only we had arrived a little earlier", said Don Octavio. "Last month we found two like that; a father and his eleven-year-old boy. They lay there, hugging. Dehydrated as they were, there were tear trails on the boy's cheeks. It was heartbreaking..."

The mental image gave me a lump in the throat; father and son forsaken together, their embrace a perfect snapshot of the moment they expired in the aggressively indifferent desert.

I guessed I was relieved that we hadn't come across a corpse on that day, although my cause for relief was really the cause for the group's feeling of failure. As the volunteers came up with conjectures to explain the disappointing find, Octavio planted the white cross firmly in the ground. Another volunteer buried a bottle of water neck deep in the soil.

"Most migrants die of issues to do with dehydration" Doña Maricela explained. "This is our way of saying; *you may rest in peace now.*"

2. Defeat.

It never became clear who had died there or who found their remains. On the way back to Ajo, I got a chance to drive with Don Ely, his wife and their close friend Don Francisco. We all discussed how the search had gone, and Don Ely chalked up the nonachievement to one of the biggest obstacles Águilas del Desierto routinely faced.

"It's very unfortunate, but there's just little to no communication with the other volunteer groups, with border patrol, with the sheriff, with the consulates... with everybody!" he lamented. "Don't get me wrong; I'm glad they found that migrant and that his family will get closure. But if that area was combed the day before, it would've been good to know. It takes a lot of time and money to organize these outings, and we rely on donations. So it's sad to discover you did a whole day's search in vain, especially if it could have been avoided with a simple heads-up."

Don Ely clicked his tongue and sighed, and his wife rubbed him on the shoulder with tenderly love. He explained how each incursion into the desert was the culmination of many days of preparation.

"We don't just show up for a hike in any random place. No. We've become very efficient at this," he said with pride.

Don Ely explained how the usual dynamic was that a family member of the missing migrant would reach out to him imploring help. This would usually happen through the Águilas del Desierto Facebook group, with over 200,000 people keeping up with the volunteers' enterprises. Don Ely would not send out a search party unless he had a solid case, that is, a more than decent amount of evidence pointing to the missing migrant's whereabouts. If the last communication from the migrant had occurred the day before, then an emergency search party could be deployed in the hopes of rescuing the migrant alive. However, if the last known information about the migrant corresponded to several days ago, then Don Ely would take the time to be more clinical about finding what at that point would most likely be a corpse. He had a long spreadsheet of people gone missing in the desert, but due to the fact that he could only afford to carry out searches on the weekends, he had to coldly choose the strongest profile on that spreadsheet every time Águilas set off.

"I have to deal with a lot of people; the migrant's families, the Indians, the army, the consulates, the coyotes…"

Don Ely unraveled how he didn't like to work with coyotes, as they were usually duplicitous and unreliable. But, every now and again, the family of the missing migrant would pressure the coyote into collaborating with the search party. Don Ely preferred not to know the terms under which these unusual arrangements occurred, but they usually involved some threat of action (be it legal or violent) being leveled against the coyote, who often hailed from the same region as the missing migrant.

"The thing about coyotes", said Don Ely "is that you can never know if they're telling the truth. They say they left the migrants some place, they say they ran to get help, they say all these things, but how can you know for sure?"

According to Don Ely, there had been cases of coyotes beating and robbing the migrants, raping them and even killing them in the wilderness. What happens in the desert stays in the desert, where the remote empty vastness offered the perfect framework to operate with complete impunity.

The army and border patrol were mostly helpful, Don Ely said, or at least they gave the idea that they wanted to collaborate with Águilas' humanitarian work.

"Although, I will say that I've ran into racist army men and border patrol officers", Don Ely pointed out. "Some really think we promote illegal immigration. Sometimes I feel like they set up traps for me, to catch me red-handed and disband us altogether. I once noticed my voice echoed during phone calls. It turned out my phone had been tapped. That explained why I had received so many mysterious calls asking me questions regarding the passage through the desert; what the best routes were, which were less sentineled, if I could recommend a coyote... Of course, I didn't answer any of those questions. Even if I knew for sure I was speaking to an actual migrant, my stance is firm: *I do not recommend or encourage crossing the desert."*

"Indians are a whole other story," he narrated. "We used to get permission from them all the time to search within their reservation, as plenty of migrants go missing there. But then, some other volunteer group left a big mess in the desert and they haven't granted a permit since."

"I think they're in cahoots with the narcos", said Don Francisco. "Think about it; they don't let outsiders in their land so that narcos and coyotes can operate in peace. The U.S. government treats the Indians like crap, so they turn to Mexicans to make a living."

"Don Francisco; your theories could make great films," Doña Maricela joked.

Don Ely lamented jumping through the usual loops of organizing a search party only to see that no result came from it.

"But I guess it evens out," Don Ely said, now with a calmer disposition. "In the same way we sometimes don't find who we're looking for, many times we find other folks we didn't set out to find."

"Once we went out looking for a corpse" Doña Maricela said "and instead of finding him we bumped into a group of eight lost migrants on the edge of death. They looked at us like we were angels. Remember that honey?",

"Yes", said Don Ely with a smile. "That was a good day."

3. Origin story.

That evening we all gathered around a bonfire at the Ajo basecamp, which sat at a slight elevation over the immensity of the desert. An army of saguaros surrounded the site, towering over us at the camp and becoming little green dashes as they stretched into the earthy horizon. I sat with Don Ely and Doña Maricela to hear the origins of Águilas del Desierto. Both of them had come from Oaxaca illegally and settled in northern San Diego over thirty years ago. Don Ely had worked all his life in construction, before a recent spine injury prevented him from carrying out arduous physical labor (such as going on the long desert hikes). Doña Maricela, who had never finished secondary education, worked as a janitor in the school district. I marveled at how the couple held such modest jobs during the week and used their weekends to venture into the dangerous desert to save lives. Águilas seemed like a valiant alter ego pulled straight out of a comic book, their normal occupations being unassuming identities to throw people off. And, like all great superhero journeys, they didn't actively pursue their calling, but rather fell into it after a tragic event transformed their lives forever.

When Don Ely first arrived in the U.S., he did so with his younger brother, Rigoberto. They lived a happy and sunny Californian life until, some twenty years later, Rigoberto was stopped at a routine border patrol checkpoint on the freeway. Upon finding out his irregular migratory status, he was deported to Mexico.

On May 16th 2009, on the day of Doña Maricela's birthday, Don Ely received a distressing call; Don Ely's brother, along with their cousin Carmelo, had gone missing while trying to reenter the U.S. through the Sonoran desert in Arizona. Don Ely began to frantically contact anybody who could help; police, border patrol, sheriffs, the Mexican consulate... However, everyone dismissed his pleas, assuring they would look into it or, conversely, that they had already done all that was in their power.

"Me humillé muchísimo," he told me. "I humiliated myself so much. I went down on my knees to beg to anyone who would listen."

Thus began a steep spiral into deep depression and torment for Don Ely, who desperately sought out clues or leads regarding his relatives' whereabouts. With the help of his teenage daughters, Don Ely learned basic computer skills for the first time in his life and began to send out emails and to investigate online. He also learned to read maps, and not just any maps, but intricate ones containing rigorous details of the desert's topography. He filled binders and pin boards with notes, schemes, calendars and reference photos. He devoted endless sleepless nights to this mad undertaking, which soon began to take a toll on his professional and personal life.

"I pleaded so much I finally was able to get a response from my relatives' coyote. He agreed to take me out to the desert and guide me to where he left my brother and my cousin," Don Ely recalled. "He did it if I promised not to sue him or anything like that after... well, after we found the bodies. I told him: 'Just take me to them and disappear from my life forever.'"

Accompanied by another volunteer search party called Angels of the Desert, the coyote took Don Ely on a long hike to the spot where he had allegedly abandoned Rigoberto and Carmelo. There were no signs of them to be found.

"He said maybe the animals dragged them away: mountain lions, coyotes, bobcats…" Don Ely said.

"Does that actually happen?" I asked.

"Yes; I've seen it. But animals are messy. They leave a trail; clothes, blood, body parts… But there was nothing like that around where we were. I was livid, because I knew the coyote was lying."

As Don Ely narrated the painful memories, he clenched his jaw with an ire that came back to haunt him from the past. He took a few seconds to breathe in deep before continuing with the story.

"I told the coyote I wouldn't rest until I found out the truth. I think he was beginning to fear what I might do."

But then something happened that Don Ely did not expect:

"A few days later he calls me up and says my brother and my cousin had been spotted in Sonoyta," he said. "I was ecstatic; it turned out they weren't dead after all. The coyote said he felt responsible for the horrible time I went through, and that he would be happy to take me to Sonoyta to find them. I was ready to leave for the border when I told my wife the good news; she stopped me dead on my tracks."

"Of course I didn't let him go," said Doña Maricela. "I told him: 'If your brother and cousin are in Sonoyta, they must know the whole family is looking for them. Why don't they call? Why don't they reach out to us directly?'"

Indeed, Don Ely had reached a point where he could not think straight anymore and was ready to hang on to the slightest thread of hope, no matter how incredible or illogical. When his wife analyzed the facts from a more removed point of view, Don Ely finally came to his senses.

"That bastard coyote and his overlords wanted my husband out of the U.S. and in their territory, Sonoyta, so they could make him disappear forever, as he was beginning to be a big pesky nuisance for them," Doña Maricela explained with sadness.

The realization that Don Ely was quite clearly being lured into a trap came with the tacit confirmation that his brother and cousin were indeed dead. Despite the fact that Doña Maricela had prevented his husband's assassination, Don Ely could hardly feel relief, as the brief moment of hope that Rigoberto and Carmelo were still alive had come crushing down like a house of cards. Don Ely's world once more became a dark, irresolvable and harrowing enigma.

Then, one day, Don Ely received a call from a man named Jaime, whom he had long tried to reach to no avail. Also a migrant, Jaime had come in the same party as Rigoberto and Carmelo, who had been one of his closest friends since childhood. Of the three, Jaime was the only one who made it to the U.S.

"Before Jaime's call, we all imagined it was my brother who had run into trouble crossing the desert, as he was a big man with diabetes," Don Ely remembered. "As it turns out, it was my cousin, younger and fitter, who had been unable to continue; he had become intoxicated from eating a piece of saguaro," Don Ely unraveled.

While it is safe to drink saguaro water in small quantities, the flesh of the cactus has acids and potent alkaloids. These chemicals are usually too acrid for most humans to tolerate and are taxing on the kidneys and stomach if ingested. Don Ely's cousin, extenuated and ravenous after days of walking, had made the mistake of munching on this poison, which can produce vomiting, diarrhea and even temporary paralysis. Physically unable to carry on, he collapsed.

"When Jaime reached this part of the story, he started sobbing. I asked him 'Why do you cry so, Jaime? Why now?' At first, he wouldn't tell me."

Don Ely paused as his eyes began to well up. He closed them gently and took a deep breath.

"But then... Jaime finally confessed that, as he began to walk away, my cousin Carmelo embraced his legs so he wouldn't leave, crying out: 'If you leave, you'll never come back, and we will die here!' Jaime looked at my cousin in the eye and told him: "I will bring back help, I promise'".

Knowingly or not, Jaime had pronounced a lie that would take away his peace for years to come. As Jaime and the coyote pressed on, the crying of his best friend faded in the distance.

"I had to let you know, Don Ely. I couldn't live with myself. I'm so sorry. I had no choice. To stay was to die as well... But I thought of my family. I had to keep moving. I'm so sorry", Jaime wept.

Only Rigoberto stayed with the ailing Carmelo. What occurred in their last moments together remains a mystery, one that ceaselessly tortured Don Ely for years. Did his cousin die first? Was his brother left stranded there with only the decaying body of his cousin? How many days did that last? When his time came, did he gradually and painlessly fade away, or did he grapple with horrifying death throes? And what was Don Ely doing while that happened? Perhaps he watched TV in his home in San Diego, perhaps he was grocery shopping or eating out with his family. Why couldn't he have been there for his brother? Why did he have to die alone, forsaken, removed from all the people he loved? Did he die in despair, or did he have time and serenity to come to peace with his destiny? Did he truly believe in an afterlife? Or fear a null black void of death that soon would engulf him forever?

With the new information Jaime provided, Don Ely set out once more into the desert. It had been four months since the migrants had been declared missing. This time, it wasn't long before Don Ely found the remains of his relatives. They were weathered, decomposed, and partly devoured by vultures and other animals. Don Ely's mind flashed glimpses of them full of life, energy and radiant happiness. Seeing them reduced to putrid corpses, semi-mummified by the desert sun, had a profoundly devastating effect on him, and one that would require years of therapy to mend. Although Don Ely and Doña Maricela recognized the corpses (and even recognized the Rigoberto's clothes), the forensic doctor claimed visual identification was at that point nonviable, given the months of decay.

"We need to run DNA tests", the doctor said. These tests, Don Ely soon found out, cost a few thousand dollars and came with plenty of bureaucratic red tape that Don Ely had nor the energy nor the resources to deal with.

"But I know that's them. I'm 100% certain. Please let me take them", Don Ely begged.

The forensic doctor suggested that Don Ely get in touch with his brother's old dentist.

"With any luck he can provide an x-ray, or even a plaster model of his denture", he said.

Don Ely did just that, and with an old x-ray of his brother's mouth, the forensic doctor was able to verify the corpse of the missing brother.

"The doctor had the decency not to have me jumping through the hoops for my cousin's cadaver as well. He released them both and we were finally able to bury them in Oaxaca", recalled Don Ely.

Don Ely presumed that obtaining a sense of closure would give him peace and that he would soon start to get back his old life. But this never happened. Don Ely couldn't sleep, and when he did, he was haunted by nightmares of his brother Rigoberto decomposing alive while crying for help.

"I was a big mess. I had lost my job. My wife had to take care of four daughters and one very depressed husband," Don Ely said, reaching out to caress Doña Maricela's hand with admiration.

Despite the fact that her birthday had become forever tainted by a tragic event, Doña Maricela soon began to see it as a providential sign. Perhaps the coincidence marked a new chapter in her life, one with unimaginable responsibility and influence in her community. What she and her husband never imagined was just to what extent their lives would now be consumed by their new calling, which would soon begin to take shape.

"My husband was in a terrible rut; depressed, unemployed, afraid... He never wanted to see the desert again. He had become pathologically afraid of it," Doña Maricela said. "But the ordeal with Ely's relatives had made him one of the most knowledgeable people for search and rescue missions in that area. He had made endless connections and had grown to know the desert passages and trails like the back of his hand. Soon, friends of friends in similar situations began to reach out to him for help", Doña Maricela recounted.

"It wasn't just that I knew the logistics well", Don Ely pointed out. "The families of missing migrants reached out to me because I knew first-hand the sort of suffering they went through."

Slowly but surely, Don Ely began to wander into the desert and face his fears for the greater good of bringing peace to another family. At first, many searches unfolded with no results. But these became few and far between as Don Ely honed his skills and learned something new every time he set out. Before he knew it, Don Ely was not only finding migrants' remains, but also saving many from almost certain death. The deep depression and pathological anguish caused by the demise of his relatives slowly began to give way to a deeper reading of the whole trial; perhaps, Don Ely thought to himself, Rigoberto and Carmelo didn't die in vain, as their deaths had resulted in the saving of many more migrants.

Volunteers were showing up in ever-increasing numbers to offer their support, and it quickly became apparent that they needed to formalize this newly established institution. *Águilas del Desierto* was founded as a 501c3 (that is, a tax-exempt charitable organization), and Don Ely was voted into the chairman position. Thus, the Oaxacan man who migrated to live the American dream in all of its riches now found a new life purpose in helping his fellow countrymen not fall prey to the same dream, which had become more and more deadly in recent years.

"Do you think the American dream is still worth it?" I asked the couple. They thought about it for a few seconds.

"There is definitely opportunity here. Yes, there is money to be made in this country. But if you ask me, as a migrant: would I come here through the desert? I would respond with a resounding 'no'. It's become too dangerous. The desert claims the lives of so many fathers, sons, brothers, and such people who come here in the hopes of sending money home."

"So... do you think if access to the desert was strictly blocked, all those deaths could be prevented?" I posed. "In other words, is the problem with the wall the fact that it isn't finished?"

Doña Maricela shook her head slowly.

"No. They'd make holes in the wall, they'd make tunnels, they'd do all sorts of things," she said. "The only effect would be the mafias would charge more, which would lead to more migrants accepting working as *burreros*, which would cause more violence... There's no solution as easy as building a wall."

I asked them if the motivations to cross into the U.S. were always matters or life and death like I had encountered in the migrant caravan in Tijuana, or if many of the migrants who didn't seek political asylum came to the U.S. with more frivolous goals in mind. Don Ely nodded and began to reflect.

"It's our own fault too. Whenever we, the Mexicans living in the U.S., return home, we can't help but flaunt our wealth to our people. It's a strange thing, because really most of us live very modestly here. But once we go down there to visit, we make a point to impress them. An expensive watch, a gold chain, an iPhone, stupid things like that. They think *'If he can have that, why can't I?'*"

"But we always tell them: *'Don't cross the desert, it's too dangerous'*", Doña Maricela explained. "And so they call us hypocrites because we are already here. They think we feel superior, and that we don't want to share a piece of this pie…"

"If only they knew…" Don Ely laughed.

He and his wife confessed to living hand to mouth in recent years, as Águilas had taken over almost their entire lives and left them with little time to earn money for the household in the increasingly costly state of California.

"It all comes down to achieving a happy, peaceful life," Don Ely philosophized. "The people that want to cross tell me; *'I'm sick and tired of living only on frijoles.'* And I tell them; *'Sure, you're eating frijoles day in day out. But you're eating frijoles with your family! Appreciate that, because the truth is, when you're in the heart of the desert alone, hot, hungry, thirsty, exhausted, injured, and with death looming around the next hill… You won't wish to be in some American city washing dishes, you'll wish to be back home with your wife and children… eating frijoles!'"*.

⌒ᕙᕗ

"It is a lot of work", Doña Maricela said the following day as we packed up to return to California. The pickup truck was filled with backpacks, coolers, tents, folding chairs, first aid kits, a grill, cleaning supplies, boxes, and countless other items needed for every expedition. The other twenty-something volunteers had already taken to the road to return to their homes in Los Angeles, Riverside, Chandler, Flagstaff, Phoenix, San Diego, etc. Don Ely and Doña Maricela oversaw that the campsite was tidied up and things were stored away and locked up before leaving. The couple, Don Francisco and I would occupy the last ride out of Ajo.

"It has taken over our lives. And it's gratifying, of course it is, especially when we rescue migrants alive," she said while the campsite disappeared behind us. "But we have sacrificed so much. We have four daughters and have missed many weekends with them over the years to come to the desert", lamented Doña Maricela, resting her head on the window as the desert passed us by along the Interstate 8.

"I'm ready to hand over the baton", said Don Ely with weary eyes. "I have done this for ten years now. It's very consuming, physically and emotionally. And California is becoming unlivable. I'm ready to return to Oaxaca. I've started moving the pieces to retire there. I will buy land and a few cattle", he said longingly.

"I have the same dream, Ely. It's the dream of anyone who's ever worked the land", said Don Francisco. "But my wife is saying she won't come with me, that she wants to stay here with the children. *Chinga su madre,* can you believe it? Obviously, she doesn't work to pay the bills like I do", he complained.

"Tough luck, Don Francisco," Don Ely replied "My *chaparrita* is coming with me to live out our golden days there."

Doña Maricela rested her head on her husband's shoulder and nodded slowly with a longing smile.

"Our girls are all off to college or working already," she told me. "We've done what we came here to do; give them more than what we got."

"Now it's time to enjoy life, to rest, to laugh, to stop feeling the pressures one feels in this country. The moment somebody steps up to replace me in Águilas, we are out of here. "

"Do you have any candidates in mind?" I asked.

Don Ely looked at me with a timid, resigned smile and shook his head slowly.

We stopped in Gila Bend to eat at roadside restaurant called Sofia's Mexican Food. It had a crummy façade with colors washed out by the sun and a neon logo covered in desert dust, but Don Ely swore by it.

"This place is great. *Bueno, bonito y barato.* Good, beautiful and cheap," he stated.

"It's not beautiful, honey" said Doña Maricela through a forced, toothy smile, patting her husband on the back as we walked into the dining area.

Don Ely and his wife ordered a *caldo de res* (beef stew), Don Francisco went for *sopes* (thick corn tortillas topped with meat) and I got the *torta de carne asada* (steak sub).

As we ate in silence, our eyes independently wound up admiring the mural on the wall in front of us. Composed of bright, glossy paint, it was an evocative landscape of a little white town perched on the top of a tall grassy mountain. A river ran through the village and continued down over the edge of a cliff, descending as a beautiful white cascade to the peaceful sea below, on which several small fishing boats floated leisurely, their peaceful wakes washing up as ripples on sandy beaches filled with palm trees. The painting was by no means a technical masterpiece, and had a crude, even infantile stroke style and composition to it. But it radiated a certain suggestive and poignant quality. It must have been alluring in a way that spoke to the heart of the patrons there, because I looked around me and saw the other people eating alone were staring at the mural with eyes that were almost gloomy.

"Where do you think that is, *cariño*?" Don Ely asked his wife.

"It's a made-up place, *amor*" she said. "But it's beautiful."

"Mmmh... It could be Oaxaca. Puerto Escondido or someplace like that", said Don Ely.

"I think it looks more like Nayarit", said Don Francisco. "We have those sorts of sights there."

"It reminds me of Livingston, Guatemala", a patron from another table pitched in. Don Francisco snickered.

"And you", he asked me, "does it remind you of home, Spaniard?"

I looked at the painting intently. It was a stretch, but I allowed myself to be carried away by the game.

"The little white village could be Andalusian. The green mountains and fishing boats remind me of Asturias. The palm trees... The palm trees are from the Canary Islands," I responded, and the mural instantly acquired a deeper reminiscent quality. Suddenly I was staring at the painting longingly as well.

"*Órale*..." sighed Don Francisco.

"And you said this restaurant wasn't beautiful", Don Ely said to his wife jokingly, nudging her gently with his elbow, as she rested her head on his shoulder.

After we ate, we stopped at a nearby station to fill up before making the long trip back to California. I asked if I could pay for the pit stop, and was vehemently turned down by everyone.

"No, no, no, no. No," Don Francisco insisted.

"But you've hosted me and fed me so gracefully. I want to contribute to Águilas. I know you run on donations", I argued.

Don Ely took me aside.

"You want to contribute? Tell the world about us. Not just Águilas del Desierto, but the migrant community at large", he said with heartfelt tone. "My people are often misrepresented. We get a lot of bad press. Other activists spite me, because I refuse to join their protests, use their hashtags, scream together... I can't do that. I can't put up a fight, because they'll shut us down. I need the people who are part of the problem to listen to me and collaborate. That's the authorities, and it's our people, the migrants", he expressed, pointing at his chest. "I have to be the bridge between the two. My hands are tied. But you? You can tell our story. Do us justice. Politics don't do much. But stories? Stories shape the world."

We drove onto the Interstate 8 once more and headed West. I had routinely driven on this highway in California to run errands in the San Diego area, and never once did I imagine that the sight of this road signaled the start of the Promised Land to so many migrants as they emerged from the physical and spiritual trials of the Sonoran Desert. The vast arid landscape looked so peaceful and so beautiful from our cushy, air-conditioned car seats. I wondered then, if in that very moment, way out there in the distance, a tired migrant meandered through the mesquites and saguaros, on the verge of collapse, feeling that every step could be his last. I wondered when he would be able to hear the hum of the distant traffic that let him know that the trek would soon be over. I wondered, or even hoped, that our very car, with its old rattling and rumbling, would contribute to that heavenly symbol of salvation.

"The desert feels so different from here. So empty of life, of stories," I thought out loud. Doña Maricela hummed in quiet agreement.

"If the desert looks empty, it's because the migrants are doing a good job..." Don Ely said with irony. "But they're out there, you can bet on that."